Life'sa beach

Life's a beach

Keep that holiday feeling all year round

Alexandra Massey

First published in Great Britain in 2008 by
Virgin Books Ltd
Thames Wharf Studios
Rainville Road
London
W6 9HA

ISBN 978 0 7535 1393 4

Mixed Sources
Product group from well-managed
forests and other controlled sources
www.fsc.org Cert no. TT-COC-2139
© 1996 Forest Stewardship Council

The Random Hou... ...rain Limited supports the Forest Stewardship
Council [FSC], the ... ...n organisatio...
All our titles that ... ...proved FSC-certified
paper carry the F... ...lo...

Our paper procur... ...ment policy can be found at www.rbooks.co.uk/
environment

Typeset by TW Ty... ...th, Devo...

Printed and boun... ...in Great Britain by
CPI Bookmarque ... ...on, CR0 4TD

1 3 5 7 9 10 8 6 4 ...

CONTENTS

INTRODUCTION: BEACH LIFE

If there's one thing in the year that we all look forward to, it's a holiday. Oh, that glorious 'sinking into the sun lounger' feeling with the sand between our toes and the sunrays feeding us large doses of happy vitamins to make up for our winter depletion. With a drink in one hand and not a worry in the world . . . It is wonderful to let go of all concerns for a week or two. No thoughts of what we've forgotten to do, what's gone wrong at work or what we meant to tell to whom. Who cares about the office politics, the lists that never got completed or those nagging doubts about the way your childcare arrangements are going? On holiday, those life hiccups seem so far away and so irrelevant to what really matters – just feeling great. The simple things can be so much fun: even food shopping is a pleasant experience, not to mention all the extra things you do on holiday, like eating out or taking a walk, which are pure joy.

But why is it that, when you return home, that holiday feeling disappears after a few days or weeks? No matter how hard you try to maintain the holiday high, it doesn't take long before you slump into the old routine and those days of pure enlightenment seem so far away. Before you know it, the whole trip seems like a dream, you are back to 'normal' and that familiar feeling of dissatisfaction creeps its way back in. It can seem that the only way to get that sense of space and freedom is to book lots of time out – then you'll be able to get back to that great feeling of being away! Realistically, it would be so much better if you had more happiness in your everyday life, rather than just waiting for those two or three weeks away on holiday.

Maybe you are now looking for something more. Do you remember your younger days when you thought you would feel free and happy at the age you have now reached? You were convinced that you would have enough money by now and your career path would be clear and that all your problems would be 'sorted' and you would be in charge of your life? Instead you find that you are a few steps behind your ambitions and you are still trying to figure out what you *really want to do*! Or you are lurching from one drama to another and feel as if it's other people who seem to be calling the shots?

Whether it's pressure at work, your children's constant demands, frustration at your partner's inability to understand you or the size of your mortgage, it's hard to see how you got here and you certainly never planned it to be this way. Perhaps you want something else, maybe more freedom or more hope. Maybe you are questioning the way it's turned out and you want more – more happiness – and this is why you have picked up this book.

There is a different way and getting there is simple but profound. If you glance around, you will see that there are some people who have tapped into that different path. These people seem to be living their life like us but also as if they were on one long holiday. They go through the everyday dramas, stresses and strains that we do, but they seem to take it in their stride and the situations that might drive you and me demented just don't seem to affect them in the same way. How do they do this?

You don't need to hide in a retreat for weeks or months or give up all worldly possessions to get that 'glad to be alive' feeling. It is accessible to anyone. It also doesn't require you to change your lifestyle: you can have the same size of mortgage, the equivalent office politics and the same humdrum routine, yet feel that life is a delight and joy comes at a moment's notice. Yes, joy at a moment's notice – it really is possible.

2

When you go on holiday, certain things happen to you that allow you to feel happy, full of fun and pleased to be there. This book will show you how you can bring that same intelligence home to get that 'Beach Life' feeling all year round. As you move through the book, it will bring your attention closer and closer, gravitating towards the profoundness that is at the centre of your capacity to feel great joy. This evolution may happen over time but it could happen very quickly. It is different with everyone, but one thing is certain: if you look in the right place, you can attain the contentment you crave.

Using This Book

The book is divided into five parts and it will look at the elements of being on holiday that affect you in a positive way and that help you to feel happier and enjoy your life more. So many of us seem to be working frantically to get ahead but don't have the time to enjoy the fruits of our diligence. The cost of this frenzied lifestyle may be that you have no time left to kick back and relax. Is it feasible to live life with more time and less stress without packing up and moving to the country? Yes, it is. And, the steps to get there are irresistibly simple.

The first part delves straight into the heart of the Beach Life philosophy by teaching you the **Stillness**. This is the name I give to the place holding the source of your joy, and it is so attainable when you are surrounded by holiday beatitude but can seem so elusive in your day-to-day life. The techniques outlined to achieve the Stillness are simple and manageable. Once you have experienced it, you will never look at your life in the same way again.

The second part answers those questions that so often come up, starting with **Yes, but . . .** and continues to explain why the Stillness will work for everyone including the person asking. The third part, '**Enjoying the Ride**', explains why you have that feeling of liberation when you're away from home. It will identify those areas that you have allowed to hold you back – for example, always feeling that you are dancing to someone else's tune or not having enough fun. This section will show you how to transform your life from an emotional

3

perspective so you will progressively guide yourself towards personal fulfilment. And the steps towards getting there are simple yet dynamic. The fourth part, '**Repacking Your Bag**', reflects on the essence of dealing with the stuff back home that trips you up. The arguments compel you to see ordinary life in a new way so that it becomes *extra*ordinary. The final part, '**Coming Home**', puts the arguments into a new perspective of living and breathing that liberated feeling without changing anything on the outside of your life.

The hardest thing to overcome in order to achieve that holiday feeling is your fettered mind. But there's no hurry, and no one waiting with a stopwatch. The philosophy of this book is drawn from the teachings of many Masters over thousands of years but is brought to you in a practical and pragmatic format.

The book's structure is designed to draw you gradually in towards true liberation, where the book will end and your Beach Life will begin.

THE JOURNEY THERE

The Stillness

You're on holiday and everything is perfect. The scenery is gorgeous, the scent of the air is exquisite, the sun is shining and you are doing exactly what you want to do. There's no routine to follow and you feel liberated, vibrant and happy to be alive. For a few moments, life is perfect and you want this feeling to go on for ever.

Look a little deeper into the 'few moments'. It's more than happiness alone: it's a path into a richer, deeper experience which feels full yet tranquil. On sensing this tranquillity for more than a 'few moments', you may sense the presence of something bigger and deeper than you normally feel. Ah! Everything is OK! It's a great feeling, one you would like to experience all the time yet struggle to maintain once you get back from holiday.

Let's cut to the chase: exactly what is at the centre of that 'holiday feeling'? It is called the Stillness. It is a silent but profound presence underneath your bubbling thoughts. It is the bliss consciousness that feels almost like another sense. It's a place where you are free of any worries. Indeed, you are free of any mental chatter. It's a glorious reunion with the deepest part of you. It's a moment of pure awareness in your true centre. This is your birthright. It is a natural state of being.

The Stillness is not a new phenomenon: it has been spoken and written about for as long as man has been on Earth. It is Zen, according to Buddhism; it is the 'Awakening' according to Sanskrit literature; and it is the 'Kingdom of God within you' according to Christian teachings. The renowned psychologist Abraham Maslow called it the 'peak experience'. He explained this experience as a feeling of pure, positive happiness when all doubts and fears were absent and weaknesses and reticence were left behind. He said it was a feeling of completeness, a feeling of belonging rather than feeling isolated as if you were outside looking in. He found that these occurrences were not limited to particular groups but happened to all sorts of people. You did not have to be special or religious to feel joy in this way.

Once you begin to feel that 'still' feeling, you will come to rely on it as an ever-present attendant. It will become the one constant in your life that you can always return to when you need solace and peace. You will begin to realise that it doesn't matter so much what goes on around you because your sanctuary is within you. You will place less attachment on outcomes. Although you will have preferred outcomes, you will not really mind what the result will be.

Everyone has Access to the Stillness

It is what connects all of us together. It's what we all have in common. You have already experienced it, perhaps only fleetingly but maybe for longer periods of time. You may have experienced it when you felt 'at one' with nature or while breathing in a spectacular view. You may have experienced it when you undertook an extreme sport, such as ice climbing, and reached the top of the thousand-metre ice cliff; the sheer magnitude of your achievement could have taken your breath away. You could have experienced it while you were holding a sleeping baby and you felt the awe of new life. Perhaps great sex was the way for you. These experiences naturally draw us into the Stillness. But if you thought it was *because* of the experience that you became aware of the Stillness then you may believe that you have to *recreate* the experience to get that wondrous moment back. But you don't.

You don't have to recreate your holiday to get that holiday feeling back.

It's Not Religious: It's Physiological

Many teachings regard the Stillness as a spiritual experience that comes from the belief of a religion, but it does not require you to believe in any religion and it is not a religious experience. If you have been on holiday and had that wonderful moment of complete bliss, it was not because you believed in a 'god': it was because you had stopped being caught up in the mental chatter that runs your mind.

How to access the Stillness comes later, but for now it is important to understand that the feelings of joy and peace are a *physiological* process and not a *mystical* experience. The problem comes in the language. Because you are not used to the language, you may find it too esoteric. This is only because these words have been linked to mystical or religious sources that may seem unfamiliar. As the human race evolves, these words will become more exoteric and more commonly used. For now, don't be concerned with the language, but understand the experience and the language will be of no consequence.

The Stillness is one term in thousands that attempt to describe something that cannot be described in words. But because the world is focused more on material gain than inner joy, the terms used for the physiological process of gaining inner joy have been left up to the mystics and not defined by scientists. If we had more scientific terms describing the procedure of touching the Stillness, then perhaps these new terms would overcome the barriers of assuming that the Stillness is steeped in religion. Even in this book some of the terms to describe the Stillness may seem a little 'hippy-dippy'. This is because our language hasn't advanced as fast as our understanding and we have to use what's both available and widely understood.

7

You do not have to believe in anything 'godly' to gain from the wisdom of the centuries. There are modern-day therapy groups that help people to go beyond thought and stress to touch the Stillness in a matter-of-fact, clinical environment. The process to do this is not magical or supernatural. The process is purely practical. We all have the potential to feel joy, but we have to be taught the steps to get there. It's not a mysterious process but it may *feel* mysterious if we haven't felt that depth of bliss before. We might think it's a 'holy' encounter simply because the feelings are so wonderfully joyous, but they are simply the feelings of contentment that we have missed because we are so tied up in modern life and its associated stress. Do you remember your parents teaching you how to touch the Stillness (or use other words to describe inner peace, contentment and joy) so that you could find a quietness from which to draw strength and happiness? Probably not – it's a rare occurrence.

What's Stopping You?

All of us have the potential to feel that holiday feeling any time we like. What stops us from feeling it is *stress* and its connection to thought. Stress has been accepted as a normal part of our lives. Many doctors believe that at least 75 per cent of modern illness is rooted in stress. That doesn't mean we have to agree to it. How much we tune into the Stillness is directly related to how much we allow our stress and thought to overtake us.

Thoughts and Stress

There is a direct link between the number of thoughts you undergo and the amount of stress you experience. This is the mind–body connection. Think about it: when you worry about deadlines, finances, other people, etc., your body gets stressed. You might get a headache, a bad stomach or something more serious. The connection is indisputable.

But, likewise, if you clear your mind of thought, you become calmer, clearer and more content. This, though, goes right against our society, which tells us that thinking is good and productive. In fact, we get paid for thinking and acting on it. But today thinking has gone beyond the productive stage and into the epidemic of 'mind racing', which is a tool we use to keep us stressed. There is a compulsion to do nothing but think, think, think – and you may find yourself feeling guilty even considering *not* thinking.

Try this now: **Stop thinking for one minute.** How easy was that? You may have found it to be near on impossible. However, you may have found that for a split second you had stopped thinking and you felt the faint brush of The Stillness. And, how long did it take you to climb back into compulsive thinking? Seconds at best?

Because of the mind–body connection, you can gauge how stressed you are by how much compulsive mind racing you are doing. If you find that you are so stressed you can't sit for more than a few minutes without reading a paper or watching some television, your mind will be a bombardment of thoughts. But in those veritable moments of bliss consciousness, because you have put aside your mental chatter, you have allowed your stress levels to drop to a minimum.

Here is a powerful visualisation to illustrate further the power of the mind–body connection:

Think about one problem that has been wearing you down for weeks. See how the stress feels in your body. Is it in your neck, stomach or perhaps at the back of your eyes?

Just for thirty seconds suspend your belief and think about the one thing you would like to happen which would resolve all your problems in an instant. Now feel your body and sense the difference. It's a big difference!

The Balance

You don't have to leave your life and meditate in a cave to feel peace and happiness and you don't have to practise accessing the Stillness all the time. As you move more towards it you will find a natural balance between the Stillness and activity, which is everything you do when you're thinking. As you tune into the resources of the Stillness you will find a peace and contentment that will pervade all your activity and simply make everything more enjoyable. You will feel more creative but more focused. You will giggle more at the commotion of life. You will be able to stand back and take a view that was once unattainable. You will feel much happier. You will laugh at yourself more. You will enjoy the very essence of life. The state at which you find yourself connected to both your outer active life and the Stillness is pure bliss.

Accessing that Beach-life Feeling

Over thousands of years Masters have shared their techniques to access the Stillness. Many of these techniques are complex and involve a lot of time, perhaps going somewhere remote for a week or two or a series of tutoring on complicated chanting to achieve that Beach Life experience. But we can't always afford the time or the money to trek off to an ashram or hole up in a meditation retreat to learn these techniques. We don't always have that commitment to ourselves and, no matter how many times we hear it's going to change our life, we are not motivated to spend the time and money.

The Stillness has been referred to in many different forms: the Divine Source, Omnipotent Presence, the Transcendent, the Almighty or the Godly inner self. However, these words conjure up celestial and intangible practices that only the very 'deep' have access to. It's a misguided image because *any* of us can practise the techniques in this book; they can be accessed immediately and are available to everyone. You don't have to 'try' and you don't have to 'make yourself' do anything.

If you did nothing else but read the **four access points** into the Stillness and left it at that, it would be enough. The essence of the whole book lies in the next few pages and, as you read the rest of the book, keep coming back to these four access points because they are pivotal for turning your life into feeling like every day's a holiday.

1. Moment to Moment

Being in the 'moment' is the most direct access point into the Stillness. This phrase is well used in spiritual and personal-growth texts but all too often it is not fully explained in plain words. Being in the moment is as it states: to be present in this second. As we grow up we are not taught this skill, and yet it is the simplest tool to slice through all of life's dramas and, in one instant, bring us to a point of joy.

What keeps you from being in the moment is your mental clutter and emotional drama. This manifests itself as anguish, stress, pressure, angst, depression, worry and fear. This is as a result of your mind's chronic racing and emotional drama. Mind racing and emotional drama go hand in hand and they need each other to keep up their momentum. They feed each other to become bigger than their sum.

But you don't have to stop them before you feel happy – it's a matter of separating them out. You can find that peaceful place yet still be fully involved in all your personal theatre. What you will find is that, as you become more integrated in the Stillness, your dramas will lessen and become less dominant. They will naturally relieve themselves of tomfoolery as you feel yourself becoming a little more objective. This replicates that Beach Life feeling when you simply allow yourself to relax and forget about your problems at home. Here's how to do it.

As you are reading this sentence, bring your attention to this moment. Not what happenend ten seconds ago; not what you have to do in a minute's time. But right now. Become aware of this moment. This may seem impossible at first but persist. Clear away all of your past and all of your future in one fell swoop. Bring your awareness into *right now*. You don't have to close your eyes: you can do it while you are reading this sentence.

You may feel the moment for only a split second, then it's gone. Don't worry. That's good enough. The split second will grow into a whole second and then into two or three seconds in a row. Whenever you remember, just come back into the moment. Not remembering you are in the moment is as good as realising you are in the moment because your awareness is right here.

Do you sense a bubbling of angst taking place in your mind? That is your life drama, it is not *you*. You (your real life) lie beneath your life drama. Can you feel the difference between the two? Can you feel the space opening up between life and life drama?

You may say, 'Yes, but, I have too many problems to worry about to be "in this moment".' Answer this question: exactly what problems do you have right now? Not problems you may have in five minutes, not something you have to attend to later tonight, but what problems do you have right now?

You don't have any problems at this second ... nothing ... in this moment ...

If you think you do, you are simply projecting a fear of the future, so come back to this moment and out of the future.

For this second, release your life drama. Everyone has life drama. *Everyone.* For this moment release it. Let it go and feel the power of this moment.

Do you feel the intensity of this moment? Do you feel the vibrancy of this second? Do you feel its wonder? Feel it, smell it, be it.

If you are still struggling to get hold of the moment, imagine the following.

Your life dramas are laid out on the kitchen work surface. There is a huge heap of stuff piled up in front of you and laid out as far as the kitchen surface stretches. The dramas of your past life are broadly stretched on your left side and your future worries are broadly stretched out on your right side.

Put your hands together at chest height. Now bring them down and push into your dramas until you feel the surface of the kitchen worktop. Gently but firmly spread your hands apart until you have created a space and you can now see the worktop.

Feel the moment as you do this. It's right there in front of you.

When you feel the joy spontaneously rise up, but only for a split second, do not despair. Whenever you remember, come back to this image and the time you stay in the moment will increase from a split second to a whole second ... from a whole second to three seconds ... from three seconds to half a minute ... and, when you get to half a minute, that is as much as you need to form a firm base on which to grow your experience of the Stillness.

The one thing that holds you back from being in the moment is your mind racing. Take another look at this mind racing and slow the thoughts down until you can get hold of them. Just as you would slow down a child's roundabout in a park. The mind racing is usually whizzing in and out of sets of 'problems'. When you were on your last holiday, how did you deal with all the 'problems' you had back home? The chances are you put them to one side and didn't let them affect you. You simply wafted them away if they came into your mind and, as the week or two went on, they seemed less and less important. You saw them more like a challenge to be dealt with and less like a personal threat to your existence.

When you arrived home you probably let them back into your life and resumed your constant mental chatter. But the 'problems' hadn't changed between your going away and coming home. What changed was that you didn't allow them to dominate you when you were away and you had a feel for your life rather than your life drama. When you came back you resumed your normal *modus operandi*. This demonstrates that you have the ability to do this again and you don't have to 'be on holiday' to achieve it.

When you focus on a problem, you are focusing on the future. You will be hoping and wishing for a certain outcome. But you have no control over a future outcome and going over and over a problem is a futile exercise. You may have something that needs to be attended to and what you do is attend to it now to the best of your ability. It's the worrying over an outcome that you cannot foresee that keeps you from the moment.

Many teachers talk of this very thing and will tell you that there are no problems or that all our problems are of our own making. This is a very enlightened approach to life and one that is hard to assimilate.

However, there is a universal truth in this philosophy which is:

When you dwell on a problem, you create an associated fear

Here is a diagram to illustrate this:

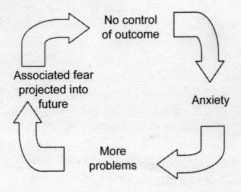

By dwelling on a problem about which you can do nothing, you create an associated fear about the future outcome and this produces anxiety, which develops into more fear and other problems. It's a vicious circle, which dominates your thinking and takes you far from the very heart of your happiness. This is what takes up the majority of your mental chatter – worrying about things you can't do anything about. How nutty is that?

If you think about all the things you are worrying about today, the chances are that you worried about 90 per cent of them yesterday and you will probably worry about 90 per cent of them tomorrow. Constantly going over and over something without putting any changes in place creates stress and fear. When you go on holiday, you let go of this chronic projection, you relax and let it go.

But now you have the tools to change that by being in the moment and doing what needs doing, now, with a focus and intent that you may never have experienced before.

2. The Warm Spot

Find a time in which you won't be interrupted. Sit in a chair that allows you to sit upright with your feet on the floor. Make sure you are relaxed. Allow your thoughts to quieten but stay focused. Bring your focus into your body. Imagine your breath entering your body. Follow the path of the breath and then visualise a continued path into the centre of your body.

Become aware of the warm spot in your body. There is one spot that is warm and glowing. This spot could be as small as a grain of sand. Focus your attention on this spot and feel how still it is. You will start to become aware of a growing warmth as you focus your attention on it. There will also be a growing 'light' emanating from this spot. Feel the warmth and the light as one. The more your attention is focused on the spot, the bigger it grows.

Stay with the warm spot and, as you do, feel it growing. It won't take long. Your attention will ignite the warm spot as a match ignites touchpaper.

Feel the energy enlarging and filling your belly and then your chest. As you keep your attention in this intensity, you will feel the light and warmth grow into your limbs, shoulders and head.

This energy takes on a life of its own. It pervades all parts of your body as if it were filling up every crevice. Imagine it moving through every digit, vein and organ like a viscous liquid. Push the liquid into every part of your body and feel each part of your body come alive as you do so. Feel the vibrations of your body. Feel the energy of your body. Drop any image you now have of your body and concentrate only on *feeling* your body from the inside.

If you suffer from mind racing, you will spend most of your time in your head. As you go over and over problems and dilemmas, you lose the sense of your body and become out of touch with how it feels to be present in your body. There lies the gap – it's in between your mind and the ground. You are hovering in the air like a hot-air balloon floating on the end of a very long rope. This can leave you feeling generally disoriented and mystified with life. Finding the Warm Spot and bringing your awareness into the body can refocus you and help you to feel more solid and stable.

When you go on holiday you are much more in tune with your body. Because you release worries and problems that keep your head buzzing at home, on holiday your attention is away from the mind and more in tune with your body. Finding the Warm Spot will help you to raise your confidence, experience an increasing easiness and joy and live a more embodied life because you are grounded in yourself and not floating outside. You will increase good feelings about yourself and you will feel more supported.

3. The Law of Nature

Do you remember being a child and feeling the world was a magical place? And it was. There were treasures to be found everywhere: watching helicopter leaves fall down from a tree, jumping into puddles, building a den or catching some creepy crawlies from the garden. All these things were daily occurrences that fostered wonder, curiosity, creativity and an eagerness to find out more. These were the gifts of childhood and they made the world seem safe and cosy.

As we grew up we lost the knack for tapping into these childhood gifts. We looked towards money, power and status to give us fulfilment. But these things never satisfied us. By tuning into the simplicity of nature, we can rediscover the ability to find the real wonders of life.

Have you ever watched a spider capture its prey in its web? It's an awesome moment watching that tiny insect conquer the huge fly and wrap it up with its sticky web strings. But have you ever watched it with children? To see their wonderment is a joy as their faces come alight with amazement. You can recapture that joy in the same way.

When you're on holiday you get a sense of that awe again. The stars seem so different from back home. The insects are unique and the plants seem alien and yet beautiful. It's so much fun trying to catch a lizard or watching out for the snakes that the locals have warned you about. You are steeped in the wonder of nature and you have stopped your mind racing. Your level of consciousness naturally comes down from your thoughts and into your senses. You are watching and looking, feeling and smelling.

Being with nature quietens the mind. It brings you down to ground level. You can almost taste the essence of life that carries on whether you are aware of it or not. But to tap into that essence awakens a joy in you that you may not have tasted for some time.

If you are lucky enough to go somewhere very quiet on your holiday, you can almost feel the Stillness. In nature the noises do not distract like cars, planes, televisions. Instead, they feel part of the greater essence of life. Listening to birds sing or watching them scratch for worms out of freshly dug soil is a reminder of where real life exists.

Close your eyes and imagine yourself in a time before humans existed. Large birds may be flying overhead while bears roam the hills looking for food. Owls would be watching from huge trees and small animals would be running around at ground level in search of their next meal. Life would be full and active. There would be noise but you wouldn't have the mind-numbing noise of modern life. There would be silences between the noises. And the noises wouldn't jar like a plane flying overhead.

The silences would be part of life, spaces in between the noises, and this is where joy lives. You would be aware of the flowing life force pervading all forms of life like a river flowing among all things. The flow of the life force links everything in nature: plants, trees, animals, birds, people, mountains, rivers, and so it goes on. It is ever changing yet still. If you bring that sense of stillness into your body you will feel the same flow running through you as it runs through all of life. This is the field of being and you can reconnect to it through the natural world. When you want to reconnect to this field of being, look up to the stars or go into the garden and immerse yourself in its wonder. Look, smell and feel all around you and allow yourself just to *be* in the ever-present stillness.

4. Waiting

Waiting is a powerful way to access the Stillness. Waiting? you ask. Don't we do enough waiting already? Maybe you spend your whole life waiting: waiting for someone else to make a decision, waiting for the lights to go green, waiting to be happy. There's waiting as in 'Hurry up, I've got somewhere to go' waiting; and there's waiting as in 'being in attendance' waiting.

Do you think of 'waiting' as an irritant you have to bear? This is modern life. Waiting is viewed as a negative: 'I was waiting around for ages!' or 'How much longer do I have to wait?' You can see other people's frustrations, in every queue, in every office or traffic jam. But what a gift 'waiting' is.

Imagine that you are watching a firework display. The biggest rocket has just been lit and whooshed up into the sky. You are waiting for the bang . . .

. . . wait . . .

. . . wait . . .

. . . wait . . .

. . . wait . . .

. . . wait . . .

. . wait . . .

. . . wait . . .

In that space between activity and activity (the whoosh and the bang) you will experience 'waiting'. Those moments in 'waiting' will draw you into the Stillness.

Move into the moment that lies in between the whoosh and the bang. It's the silence in between your thoughts. It's a stillness that is like no other. It's the richness of your full potential. It's omnipresence. It is a sense that you can be present in every place at any time. The experience of waiting is not bound by anything. It is beyond our understanding and our language. It has to be experienced before it can be understood.

But it is a very simple technique. You do not have to undergo a course to acquire it. It's so simple you might miss it.

And, as you 'wait', you will feel your perception become acute. Your natural emission of consciousness from the very centre of you will develop as you become more and more rooted in your body. You are like a battery that is charging up and sending the light of the torch into the whole body with a stronger and stronger beam. In this place you cannot help but feel the bliss of your complete presence.

You will not be thinking or anticipating your next move. You will be totally absorbed into what is happening in this moment. Your attention will filter out from your nervous system, into your senses and then into your experience. This is a natural process that our mind-numbing existence has forgotten about. The reawakening of your present consciousness will encourage this state of being more and more often. It is subtle yet magnificent and once you have experienced it you will want to be there more and more.

'Waiting' encourages an awakening of a part of you that was asleep. This mechanical technique jump-starts a whole inner awake-ness maybe you didn't know you had. It is a state of restful alertness when the thinking process has become almost zero. You will find that, when you come back into thought, you have a clarity and perception not previously there. As with an archer who pulls back the bow, the arrow will travel with more speed and accuracy. Yet there is no intellect required to pull back the bow, just the prising apart of the past and the future to find the present moment.

Whenever you find yourself in a queue, instead of fretting to get to the front, 'wait' in line. If you have no control over your allotted place in the queue, then practise this technique. Waiting in line, in a traffic jam or on a train will become a perfect moment to reach into the Stillness. You may as well. What else is there to do? You will find yourself at the front of the queue with greater ease and clarity.

This is similar to what you experience on holiday. Waiting for a train or boat when you are away is different from waiting back home. Because you have left your to-do lists behind, together with the politics and your email's inbox, you simply drift into just being there. You look around and take in the unfamiliar culture, the smells and the people. You don't really mind so much when there's so much to enjoy. And, by practising the technique of 'waiting' in your everyday life, you can get into that holiday mode and enjoy limitless joy.

You Don't Have to Give Anything Up

Have you ever picked up a great-looking book that promised you peace and fulfilment? And then you read on – and it tells you how much time you have to put aside each day to achieve it? And how many weeks you must practise the techniques before you can hope for a glimmer of 'Zen-ness'? Your heart sinks because you know that, in spite of all your good intentions, you're just not realistically going to achieve that. You have loads of goodwill but not loads of time.

Achieving the Stillness doesn't require you to give up anything, because you are not replacing anything or pushing anything aside. There's no need to stop what you're doing and concentrate. You don't have to change the way you work or relax. It's not necessary to move to the country, give up your mad friends or leave the kids with someone else. Here is a list of what you *don't* need to give up:

- job
- goals
- relationship
- friends
- time
- solace
- happiness
- debts
- sex
- children
- depression
- humour
- illness

- drinking
- moodiness
- partying
- passion
- creativity
- mortgage
- pill popping
- laziness
- having fun
- feeling bad
- pets
- obsessions
- exercise

- stress
- love
- quietness
- cynicism
- spending money
- messing about
- sport
- competitiveness
- eating junk
- peace
- laughing

'Life matter' is all the stuff we think that keeps us from the moment. It's the planning, forward thinking, worrying, fearing, regretting, dramatising, yearning, wishing and so on that keep us swept up in 'life matter'. We have forgotten that our life sits just under the surface.

Life's a beach

As you bring your focus into the moment while going about your normal life, you will prise apart the 'life matter' that sits on top of your life. While your mind is racing in all directions, you may forget to do this, but, as soon as you remember, just bring your mind into the moment again. This is where the phrase 'moment by moment' is derived from. You may get a sense of the Stillness for only a fraction of a second. Do not fret. It's a simple practice that will stretch that split second into a whole second. Then you begin to stretch the moment from a whole second to a whole five seconds.

Give Up Nothing

The reason you give up *nothing* is so you never attach positive changes that you experience to giving up *something*. It's not necessary to give up anything, so you carry on your normal life but bring your focus more and more into the moment. If you are gambling on something outside of yourself to bring you happiness – a new house, a publishing deal or a new job – and you get it while putting into practice the principles of the Stillness, then you may always associate the profound life changes with that outside 'success'.

By giving up nothing, you don't attach the Stillness to anything outside yourself.

A New Sense of Awareness

As these changes take place within you, your outer world will naturally change. The changes are so profound that it's tricky to put the transformation into words. Each person experiences it in a personal way. But, as an overall description, it's as if you have opened the door to a house that has been locked up for a long time. The air inside is musty but, as the fresh air flows in, it naturally pushes the stale air out. As the fresh air blows through the house there is less and less mustiness. It's a sense that cannot be 'thought', only felt. It's a shift from stress, numbness and fear to a sense of aliveness and oneness, a radiant energy that pervades everything.

A Stress-busting Meditation

From Outward-bound to Homeward-bound

Outward-bound: Can you think back to your last holiday and remember how you felt on your way there? You may have packed in a hurry or had been finishing last-minute jobs that left you feeling speedy and a bit frantic. Perhaps children had not behaved as planned and you had a few tears before you finally got everyone in the car. As you drive off you realise you've left some gadgets on and you have to go back to switch them off. Now you're late, your mind is racing and your heart is pounding.

Homeward-bound: It's the journey home and you've left your holiday destination feeling relaxed and happy; you've had a great time and you feel calm and clear. While your mind is in 'idle' you begin to think of some new plans you might like to put in place at work or home. Perhaps good ideas are flowing and that makes you feel refreshed and renewed.

We're all familiar with these different states of mind. This meditation helps your mind to settle down from the outward-bound state to a homeward-bound state – a more peaceful state – while keeping you clear and alert.

Find a comfortable place to sit. Make sure your spine is erect and your feet are on the floor. Close your eyes.

Turn your attention to your breathing. Breathe naturally and gently through your nostrils. Become aware of the sensation of your breath. Bring your attention towards the breath but don't try to control your breath. Be aware of it as it enters your nostrils and then leaves through your nostrils.

Do you have thoughts come up? This is normal. When you realise that you have some thoughts, gently return your attention to your breath. Don't try to control your thoughts. Don't try to stop your thoughts. Simply allow them to float away and return your attention to the breath. Return to the breath with delicacy. Make it unhurried and light. Keep it easy.

Do this for ten minutes (you can use a clock or watch) and then stop focusing on the breath. Allow yourself two minutes of rest time before you slowly open your eyes and get up. You can build up to twenty minutes, twice a day as you feel the benefits.

This meditation allows you to flow with the natural tendency of the mind rather than trying to make it concentrate. This is a replication of the homeward-bound feeling you will have when returning from your holiday. The meditation replicates the stress leaving your body through thoughts.

This meditation is for releasing stress and it's how you feel *after* the meditation that counts, not how you feel *during* the meditation. It's like exercising: you may not get the full benefits of your efforts until after the exercising has finished. If you feel that you have so many thoughts that you can't concentrate, that's OK. The thoughts are a form of stress release. And, when you become aware of your thoughts, simply come back to your breath. The way that this meditation works allows your stress to release itself through thoughts. All you have to do when you realise you have thoughts is to come back to your breath. Don't follow your thoughts and pay no attention to their meaning. Just come back to your breath. But don't force anything. It doesn't matter where your thoughts have taken you – simply return to your breath.

This meditation is simple yet profound. If you find that you cannot close your eyes for even ten minutes, just do it for a few minutes. Always rest for two to three minutes after you have stopped bringing your attention to your breath. The meditation will not make you *more* agitated – it is simply highlighting how agitated you already are. As you find that thoughts race into your mind, don't fret: this is a sign of stress release. Don't fight your thoughts: simply return to your breath.

Some people think that meditation should engender no thoughts or feelings, but nothing could be further from the truth. As long as you are alive you will have thoughts and feelings.

When you begin to meditate you may find that your thoughts run riot, like huge waves, and have become even more feral than before. Don't worry, this is normal and it's a good thing. What's happening is that you have become quieter rather than that your thoughts have become wilder. In your quietness you have become more aware of how noisy your thoughts are. Don't fret but keep meditating, keep returning to your breath whenever you remember and allow your thoughts to come and go without attaching yourself to them.

Likewise, do you find yourself feeling tired while you meditate? It's not the meditation that's making you feel tired: it is that you are becoming *more aware* of how tired you feel. There's nothing for you to do except catch up on your sleep! If you fall asleep while you are meditating, that's OK. Simply take a few moments with your eyes closed after you wake up to give yourself time to come out of the meditation again.

If you practise this meditation you will calm your mind to a point when you find thoughts will gradually subside and this will leave you with that homeward-bound feeling. Think of yourself as a lake. The surface of the lake represents our thoughts. The depth of the lake represents the Stillness. If there are many ripples on the surface of the lake, then thoughts are bubbling up from the springs deep below. You cannot stop the bubbles rising, nor would you want to. As the bubbles of thought rise and leave the lake, the depths of the lake settle down from a murky rumbling to a clean, even sediment. The more you allow the bubbles of thought to rise through meditation, the more even, settled and less stressed you will feel after your meditation.

UNPACKING YOUR BAG – YES, BUT I CAN'T, BECAUSE . . .

You've read the Stillness, you've taken in the four access points and you understand the idea that you don't have to give up anything, but you're still saying to yourself, 'That's all very well but it doesn't apply to me. *I* can't be happy because . . .'

This section is for you. The reasons we tend to give for not being able to feel that life's a holiday are all part of life's drama, and as a result we endure persistent mind racing. Even though the Stillness lies beneath the dramas and mind racing, it helps to get the dramas in perspective so they take their appropriate place in the bigger scheme of things. This section looks at the most common reasons we cite for not being happy and observes them from a different standpoint.

I'm Not Happy in My Relationship

'Love is the irresistible desire to be irresistibly desired.'

Mark Twain

Do you go away on holiday, away from the stress and strains, and you and your lover finally get on after months of niggles and of feeling stuck and dissatisfied? The break away from daily life irons out those creases of tension. It's good to be relaxing together for the first time in ages. The change of scenery, fine food and rest can bring out a whole new side of a partnership that you might have forgotten about.

But on your return you found those feelings evaporated. Give it a couple of weeks and you might as well not have had a holiday. You slump into the post-holiday blues along with the post-romance blues. Where do those loving feelings go? Have you become so caught up in what's going wrong in your relationship that you feel you are unable to be happy until things change? And, more often than not, that means the other person has got to change. In other words, *if only he/she would change then I would be happy*!

Maybe you have been waiting to meet 'the one' before you feel happy. You are not alone. There is a universal myth that finding the right lover is the path to wholeness and true bliss. We are fed this idea from birth. The classic fairytale tells the story about the Princess being rescued and swept up by the handsome Prince; they ride off together into the sunset and live happily ever after. As adolescents we listen to love songs that teach us a fairytale from the same sacred writ. Lyrics such as 'You know I can't live without you' or 'You are everything and everything is you' or 'I've got a crummy job / it don't pay near enough / to buy the things it takes / to buy me some of your love' continue to feed the fairytale. We search for our true soulmate and we think that, until we find them, we can't be happy.

If you think you may be resting your happiness on a relationship, take a look at these myths and truths and see if any apply to you. With each one you will find a quick checklist that will help tell you which of these *myths* you believe in followed by a *truth* and the *cure*.

Four Relationship Myths

'Piglet sidled up to Pooh from behind. "Pooh!" he whispered. "Yes, Piglet?" "Nothing," said Piglet, taking Pooh's paw. "I just wanted to be sure of you."'

A A Milne

Myth 1: I'm OK Only When I'm in a Relationship

Have you ever experienced the deeply satisfying feeling of 'love'? The love that overwhelms you when you enter into a new relationship? The love that makes you feel as if you could change the world? This is called 'Dream Love'. You feel alive, warm, whole and special. Your feelings are linked to the other person so much that you *crave* to be with that person so you can feel vibrant and alive again. You feel that you can conquer anything life throws at you, as long as you are together. The feeling is so strong it acts like a length of rubber drawing you back towards your lover. You feel that a part of you is missing when you are away from your partner, leaving you insecure, lonely and a little frightened, and that you'll not survive without them.

The Dream Love sensation is so powerful that you are bonded to your partner. It solidifies your identity. It helps to turn you into the person you think you are – a part of another person. It has produced a 'safe' place and you feel comfort in the easiness of your relationship and you feel threatened if this safe place is disturbed. These feelings can feel so strong that they seem 'magical' and you believe that, if you hang on to that feeling, all your troubles will go away.

Perhaps that romantic holiday helped to ignite those feelings again and, for that magical week, you were dancing on air. But when you got back you settled back into life's routine and you lost those magical feelings. You may have felt as though your lover had 'abandoned' you or you just don't know if this is the right relationship for you. Frankly, you knew the good stuff wasn't going to last for long. It can become an obsession that swings between 'can't live with them' and 'can't live without them'.

But hang on! Before you make the decision to give up on happiness because your relationship isn't perfect, pose this question to yourself: am I relying on a relationship to make me feel OK? It's a common theme – believing that a relationship can 'fix' you and your feelings and 'make' you happy. It's not possible, but that doesn't stop millions of people expecting otherwise.

The checklist

Here is a checklist to establish whether you rely on being in a relationship to feel OK.

- You don't feel happy with yourself.
- You feel scared at being on your own.
- You constantly compromise yourself to keep the peace.
- You feel something is wrong with you.
- You lose interest in your own life and friends when in a relationship.
- You worry about the other person leaving . . .
- . . . but feel trapped.
- You cannot leave the relationship without overlapping with a new one.
- You know your relationship doesn't work but you stay anyway.
- You don't think you can take care of yourself.
- You have difficulty saying no when your lover asks you to do something.
- You feel selfish when you put yourself first.
- You feel responsible for your lover's wellbeing.
- You feel good only when your lover praises you . . .
- . . . but criticism from your lover feels threatening.
- When you're upset you think it's their fault.

If you have answered yes to any of these then you do rely on being in a relationship to make yourself feel OK.

'I'm not happy with him/her but I can't live without him/her.' It's a stock phrase but well used if you are in a relationship because you are too scared not to be.

The truth is you don't need another person to make you feel complete, whole or fulfilled. A good relationship doesn't *make* your life: it *enhances* it. When you are in a relationship to prop yourself up, you invite people to treat you disrespectfully, which reduces your own sense of worth. Your neediness increases and you become more insecure and the whole cycle escalates into a sequence of trying to please, getting angry, feeling depressed and then becoming even needier.

If you believe that you are whole only when in a relationship with someone else, you may have fallen for the myth that 'love conquers all'. This is called Dream Love. The feelings that accompany the falling-in-love stage are like a powerful drug that bonds us to our lover. It is an important part of our love ritual. But it is a temporary phase and the strength of those initial feelings will fade. While this phase of the relationship takes place it helps us unconsciously to agree terms and references for the rest of our time together, such as relationship rules and roles, weighing up moral and spiritual values, negotiating future aims and ambitions to see if they match with each other – and so forth. A bit like a moral contract.

But, if you are in this relationship because you need to be with another to feel at one with someone else, then you are living in a state of dependency. No relationship can sustain the Dream Love for ever. While the Dream Love appears to offer freedom from all the insecurities that you have, you may also be aware that this state of being disguises your own neediness, insecurity about your own worth, anxiety about being lonely and feeling incomplete without the other person. If the Dream Love state begins to disintegrate, you may find yourself clinging on to your lover because the very essence of who you've become is at risk.

The truth: you don't need a relationship to feel OK
Once the Dream Love phase has worn off, the true work of any relationship begins. As the Dream Love dissolves and the relationship settles down, a separation happens. This separation is a healthy rediscovery of your needs and feelings. It's a recommitment to yourself to look out for your good feelings rather than depending on someone else to give them to you. You learn to solve your own problems and in turn your self-trust will take root and grow.

Emotional separation doesn't mean the end of the relationship: it means the beginning of a new one. As you release the need to cling to the relationship in order to 'make' you happy, you will allow your lover the space to concentrate on his/her own needs and feelings. It's a coming together of a more enlightened relationship through a new strength and self-care.

The cure
The cure is fivefold:

1. **Make yourself happy:** When you are thinking, 'What can I do to make him/her happy?' turn that thought around and ask yourself that same question: 'What can I do to make *myself* happy?' You have much more potential to make yourself happy than anyone else. Don't give anyone else that responsibility.
2. **Approve of yourself:** Likewise, when you are thinking, 'Does he/she approve of this?' turn it round and ask yourself if *you* approve of this. You will start building strength in your own moral standards.
3. **Nurture that lonely part of you:** When you need to feel cherished, give it to yourself before you go in search of it from another person. This takes the heat out of your request and the other person may be more able to respond to you because you don't seem so deprived.
4. **Start to trust yourself:** When you're dying to ask, 'Do you think that's a good idea?' ask yourself first and get your own answer before you ask your lover. This lessens the impact their answer will have and you won't feel so flattened if they say no.
5. **Practise moving into the Stillness at a moment's notice:** Whenever you feel wobbly, simply touch the sanctity of the moment and you will notice how this practice brings a certain comfort and security that will replace your yearning and dependence.

Myth 2: I Am Responsible for My Partner

It's lovely to do things for your lover: make a good meal, take them shopping, bring home a surprise bouquet of flowers. But this behaviour can tip into a powerful feeling of responsibility of your partner's actions, thoughts and feelings. You may think you even need to *rescue* your partner if you think they are unhappy, angry or depressed. You may feel that it's up to you to fix it for them because they seem insecure or out of their depth.

The checklist
Here is a checklist to see if you feel responsible for your partner.

• You finish your partner's sentence.
• You think you know what they're thinking.
• You solve their problems.
• You protect them from people.
• You say yes when you mean no.
• You do things without being asked.
• You anticipate their needs.
• You do more than your fair share.
• You feel bad or sad when they feel bad or sad.
• You feel an urgency to take away their pain.
• You feel guilty if you can't.
• You feel on a high when you've fixed them.

If you have answered yes to any of these, then you feel responsible for your partner

The truth: you are not responsible for any other adult
Unless you have a legal obligation to look after another grown person, you are not responsible for any other adult. If you think you *are* responsible, this is because you are inadvertently trying to quell your own anxieties by pacifying your lover's needs. For example, if your lover was depressed and you found yourself trying to talk them through it or trying get them some help, you are possibly trying to fix them so they don't abandon you. If your lover was unconfident about meeting people at a social outing and you stayed close to them to

protect them from their own insecurities, you may feel good because you 'saved' them, and this will release an upsurge of powerful feelings.

In fact, if you think you *are* responsible for your partner's feelings, you have given yourself more power than any human being can possibly have because no one can climb inside another person and change the way they feel – it's impossible. If your lover is telling you that you 'made' them feel angry or sad, it is an untruth. We cannot 'make' anyone feel a certain way; likewise, we cannot 'fix' their feelings.

Equally, your feelings are not the fault of anyone else. If you let those words sink into you, right now in the moment, you will sense the incredibleness of these words.

You are not responsible for anyone else's feelings and no one is responsible for yours.

The liberation that arises from this knowing is the beginning of self-freedom that feels like an intense presence of the moment, which can take you into another realm.

The cure
The cure is fivefold:

1. **Put yourself first:** When you find yourself worrying about another person, stop and ask, 'How do I feel?' This will bring you out of their space and back into your own.
2. **Start with 'I':** When you talk to another person, change your statements from 'you always' and 'you never' to 'I feel' or 'I think'. This will shift your focus from someone else's viewpoint/feelings to your own. Not only does this stop you feeling responsible but it also helps you to understand what you want or feel
3. **Define your responsibilities:** Make a list of what you need to be responsible for. This helps apportion *appropriate* responsibility to you and leaves room for your partner to take up their responsibility.

4. **Say no, not yes, if you don't want to do something:** You
   may face an uprising in the ranks, but stand firm. You don't have
   to be aggressive but be assertive.
5. **Practise moving into the Stillness at a moment's notice:**
   Whenever you're about to take up responsibility for another, bring
   yourself back to the moment and giggle at yourself and your
   incessant need to be all-powerful. Embracing the moment will put
   your responsibilities into perspective.

Myth 3: If I Change, then Maybe He/She will Love Me More

Do you feel insecure in your relationship with your partner and think
that, if you change into the person that they want you to be, then, and
only then, will you be lovable? You may think that if you 'look' a
certain way or 'act' a specific way then maybe you will get someone
else to love you. You could be demanding perfection in yourself in
order to attract the right response from your lover.

The checklist

Here is a checklist to see if you try to change yourself to attract love.

- You 'beat yourself up' in your mind.
- You shame yourself for saying, acting, feeling a certain way.
- You tell yourself you don't matter.
- You have to achieve something to be liked.
- You can tolerate lots of negative feedback.
- You try to avoid shame by being perfect.
- Your expectations of yourself are incredibly high.
- Negative criticism feels like an attack on you.
- You nag others because you do it to yourself.
- You say yes when you mean no.
- You struggle to enjoy life.

If you have answered yes to any of these you probably change yourself
to attract love.

The truth: you cannot 'make' your lover love you more

No matter how much you try, you cannot make anyone love you. This is delusional thinking. While being on that beach you and your lover may have been so relaxed that the time spent together seemed perfect. You had their full attention and you relished being the centre of their consideration. On returning home, you both return to the patterns you left behind and suddenly that good feeling has gone. Your lover goes back to work and you go back to trying to be perfect for them.

It takes only a shift of thinking to readjust this common practice.

The cure

The cure is sixfold:

1. **Tell yourself you are beautiful:** It may be uncomfortable at first but don't give up. Beautiful people tell themselves that, and that's why they're beautiful.
2. **You are wonderful:** This is in spite of all your foibles and idiosyncrasies. You are perfect because of your eccentricities. Accept them as part of you.
3. **Don't be tough on yourself for your mistakes:** Relax and learn from them. People who are confident have made loads of mistakes and this, in turn, has made them comfortable.
4. **Don't allow yourself to be treated unkindly:** You have as much right to respect as anyone else on this planet. Do this and you will feel more loved.
5. **Cherish yourself with all your heart:** You are not a mistake: you are gorgeous. Your life will become easier as you do this.
6. **Practise moving into the Stillness at a moment's notice:** Whenever you're about to change yourself to get attention, bring yourself back to the moment and feel that unbounded and abundant self-love.

Myth 4: If Only My Partner Would Work Less/Pay Me More Attention/Stop Drinking so Much, then I Would be Happy

You may have got yourself into that mode of thinking that your identity is based on someone else's behaviour. 'As soon as they change their way, then I can afford to relax into that Beach Life I yearn for.' You may be trying everything to get them to change. Screaming, crying, manipulating, bullying or pleading. Do you recognise any of these?

You may blame them for *ruining* your life or stopping you from doing what you really want to do. You could be obsessed with the other person's actions and you just can't get your mind off them for one minute even to think about 'having a moment'. You may be wishing, wishing, wishing: *I wish he would give up gambling . . . she could stop drinking . . . he could get a better job . . . she were nicer to my friends . . . then I would be happy.*

The checklist

Here is a checklist to see if you are waiting for someone else to change before you can be happy:

- You think they should do it differently.
- You worry incessantly.
- Being obsessed keeps you balanced.
- You can't let go.
- You know only how they are feeling, not your own feelings.
- You react instead of respond.
- You pander to their whims.
- You feel out of control.
- You can't see the wood for the trees.
- You feel tired much of the time.

If you have answered yes to any of these you are probably waiting for someone to change for you to be happy

The truth: you do not have to wait for anyone else to change for you to be happy

You do not need to wait for the people around you to change before you can get the happiness you are looking for. If you wait for your lover to change, you will be waiting for ever. If you are in the mindset of waiting for your lover to change before you can feel contentment and fulfilment, then you are holding yourself from your true potential. It's no different from 'When I get there, I'll be happy' or 'When I earn this much, I'll be happy.'

If someone is behaving in a way that is detrimental to you, you have two choices: you accept their behaviour or you leave the situation. What else is there? It is not possible to change another human being, no matter how hard you try; it is a futile exercise. Think about it: how long have you tried?

But, while you are deciding what action to take, relinquish your judgements. Judging another person is stressful. As long as you are judging someone you are placing yourself on a pedestal from which you decide what constitutes human perfection. It's hard work trying to be perfect and it will wear you down.

The cure

The cure is sixfold:

1. **Gently separate yourself:** But do this with love. This leaves both of you being responsible for themselves.
2. **Stick to what's yours:** Don't take on another's responsibilities. This releases you from unnecessary burdens.
3. **Allow them to be:** In turn you will allow yourself to be. You don't have to wait for anyone else to offer you freedom from obsession.
4. **Stop creating more chaos:** And learn to become more present. This will enable you to make better decisions.
5. **Release guilt about not doing enough:** You don't need to do any more. This will bring you calm.

6. **Practise moving into the Stillness at a moment's notice:**
Whenever you find yourself trying to get someone else to change,
bring yourself back to the moment and feel the release of
obsessions and the pure joy that brings.

Let the Light into Your Relationship

As you begin to 'let go' of the other person in your life and consciously
bring your centre of attention into the moment, you will feel the
growing light of your own being. This is the way to develop your
relationship and get more of that Beach Life feeling. The more you
grow the light inside you, the more you will brighten the light in your
relationship, even if the other person doesn't change. You will see
them in a different way, needing less from them and expecting less of
them.

In a relationship where the two parties are highly dependent on
each other, there is an overlap which is called 'enmeshment'. Here's
an illustration.

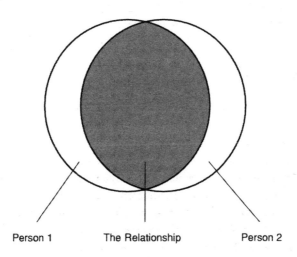

Person 1   The Relationship   Person 2

Life's a beach

In this diagram there are two people who are overlapping (enmeshed) and the area where they overlap is the relationship. You can see that the two people are on top of each other, leaving little room to grow individually.

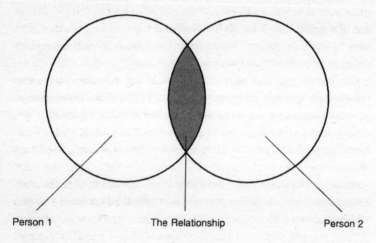

Person 1   The Relationship   Person 2

In *this* diagram, however, you can see the separateness of each person, which allows lots of input into the relationship without overwhelming both people.

Moving into the Moment

When you move into the moment, the separateness will happen naturally. You will begin to disassociate with the quirks that create disharmony, such as conflict and pain. As you start to accept the other person for who they are rather than what you want them to do for you, you will see them as distinct from you. The frustration you have experienced while trying to change someone else will subside because your focus will change. The pain you have experienced while trying to get something from someone who hasn't got it to give will dissolve because you are giving it to yourself. You will need less approval from others and gain the ability to give more to yourself. This will leave you feeling more fulfilled and contented.

As you let go of judging your partner and accept them for the person they are, you will stop the incessant conflict you have inside. Judging others creates frustration in yourself because, when you try to change someone, you only end up banging your head against a brick wall. Accepting others and their idiosyncrasies, even if you do not like them, shines a new light on your relationship, which will in turn *lighten* you. As you criticise your lover less, they will lower their defences and allow more fun back in.

Can you see the new pattern forming? No matter that you want to leave/break up/run a mile sometimes, before you make any decisions, practise lowering your judgements and criticisms of yourself, then others, and let the lightness back into your relationship. Once you have achieved this, you are ready to make a decision about the future of your relationship. If you practise moving into the present, love and acceptance will stay with you whether in this relationship or the next. You may as well challenge your ability to be the best lover you can while in this relationship to avoid the same tendency in another. Indeed, you can address the inadequacies of 'the relationship' through the inadequacies of yourself, and if you heal yourself, the relationship will flower into its true potential. The love you have for another person lives inside you. You can only love someone else based on how much you love and respect yourself.

I'm Too Ill

'The statistics on sanity are that one out of every four Americans is suffering from some form of mental illness. Think of your three best friends. If they're okay, then it's you.'

Rita Mae Brown, author

Perhaps you are ill and you just haven't got the mental energy to be bothered with getting that Beach Life feeling. Then again, you *are* reading this book and so perhaps you want to change something but the change feels like hard work. If you have a long-term illness, have you ever stopped to consider how your mental health and emotional wellbeing may be impacting on your recovery capability?

Stress Overload

It is more and more commonly thought that many illnesses are a direct result of an overload of stress. This is not surprising given the incredible pressures we put ourselves under in order to 'get on'.

When tension and stress build up, this is felt throughout the body. You may feel the build-up of stress in your neck, through your back muscles or as a headache. This is undisputable.

There's more on stress under 'I'm too stressed' below.

Mind, Body, Spirit

Thoughts affect the emotions and the emotions affect the body. There is a powerful link between the mind, the spirit and the body; therefore, it could be argued that what you think manifests itself in how you are physically. Likewise, how you are physically manifests itself in how you think. If you feel physically good, you think good thoughts and have a sense of wellbeing. Equally, if you feel physically bad, you have negative thoughts and have a low mood.

You may be constantly aware of an anxiety in your mind and this can be exhausting and a constant irritant to the nervous system. As with a maid whose mistress is continually changing her mind as to what she wants done, and where and how, it will leave the servant stressed, anxious and irritated. It can tip into exhaustion and illness. This is not to say that it's the reason why you are ill but the very illness itself may be playing on your mind and hindering your recovery.

Working from the Inside Out

A good gardener will notice when his plants, trees or shrubs are unwell. Gardeners generally *don't* apply the Western medicine hypothesis to a sick plant by attending to the dying leaves or wilting bloom by placing chemicals on to its outer layer. They are more likely to look at the underlying causes of the illness and treat it accordingly by nourishing it from within – from the roots up.

Letting Go

If you are ill it could be that you are trying to 'hang on'. Perhaps you are worrying about what you can't get on with because you're incapacitated. But it could be that your illness is your body telling you to 'let go'. When you are incapacitated it feels as if you are in the bedroom cupboard and everyone else is in the kitchen. You know there's activity going on out there but you just can't get to it. If you stop trying to get to the activity you are left alone with your illness. Can you use this time to let go and just be? Can you allow yourself to be with yourself and give your body the time it needs to heal?

Resolving Pain

Sustained attendance in the moment will help to dissolve the emotional pain. By dissolving emotional pain you will be unhooking yourself from the chains that keep you in the role of 'victim' to your illness. And, by severing these hooks, you will be allowing yourself the freedom to make better choices for your recovery. Indeed, illness gives us an incredible opportunity to 'let go' and resolve emotional pain. Your body has given you a signal to slow down and take stock, and the art of utilising this time is to let go and just accept it as it is.

Bring it into the moment

As you bring yourself into the moment, you may feel more pain than before. This may be an internal struggle because you have never felt pain 'in the moment' before. Stay with it, because the light of your consciousness will ease the pain. If you have never experienced this you may be sceptical, but there is no better time to experience this than now. Yes, it may feel uncomfortable to start with but that is

43

because you are climbing the last peak of the mountain range before you have seen the view at the top. Don't stop just because you want to slide back into the denial of your pain. Stay with the light of your consciousness and you will feel the pain dissolve.

Radiating Joy

Have you ever heard the phrase 'what you focus on grows'? When you learn to fly a paraglider, you are taught only to look at where you want to go. If you focus on the gorse bush on the side of the hill that you just know you are going to hit, and it's now jumping all over the hillside in order to get in your way deliberately and distract you from where you should be going, and it's growing bigger and bigger in front of your eyes until it's the size of a house, and then – *bang*! You are stuck in it and you're so stunned you haven't a clue what you've broken, how scratched to pieces you are and what your name is! Fear steered you into that bush. Because you focused on it, fearing you would end up in the middle of it – you simply flew straight into it. Then again, if you ignore the side of the hill and focus on the soft green field below you, you will gradually drift down and gently land on the exact spot that you were aiming for.

Likewise, if you focus on how bad you feel while you're ill you will feel worse. Conversely, if you focus on the moment, you will feel the radiance of your consciousness light you up from the inside out, which will send a pure warmth throughout your whole body. Think of a small baby being attended to by its mother. When the mother gives her full attention to the baby, the baby radiates joy. Our spirit is as pure as a baby's and to give it our full attention is to allow it to radiate with joy.

If you are ill while reading this, you may as well make the most of the moment. Each time you remember, bring your conscious mind into the Stillness. Allow the space in between your thoughts to arise and expand. Consider your illness a gift of *lost time* in which you may be in the moment without any distractions. Surrender to this moment.

I'm Too Stressed

'Stress is who you think you should be. Relaxation is who you are.'

Chinese proverb

How are things, then? 'Oh, I'm stressed out. I guess I'm trying to do too much.' A common answer. The surveys tell us that 40 per cent of us feel under constant pressure, are running behind and struggling to stay in control. Stress is on the increase; millions of work days are lost to it; it's produced a multimillion-pound industry to combat it; and we've probably felt it at least once today.

It's as if we'd been infiltrated by an unseen force and it were growing inside us all the time. It's become so normal that we accept it as part of life. So much so that, if we're with someone who is chilled and relaxed, we might think, 'What's wrong with them?'

But, thankfully, for one or two weeks a year, we can put the stress aside because the holiday is here. We sit by the pool or get out on the piste and *phew*! – no more stress until we get home. We are not going to let our job, debt, family politics or whatever get to us while we're here. We are going to put it out of our minds and enjoy ourselves. And, when we get back, we are going to hang on to that lovely holiday bliss and not let the grind get to us.

Does this happen to you? You may find your resolve strong on your return from your holiday, but, without your noticing, stress crept back in and you're back to 'normal' – stressed out and not getting that Beach Life feeling. Here is a checklist to see how much stress you are under.

How vulnerable are you to stress?
(Courtesy of the Stress Manangement Society)

Mark each statement from 1 (always applies to you) to 5 (never applies to you), according to how accurate each statement is in describing your current lifestyle.

	Always applies				Never applies
	1	2	3	4	5
I get seven to eight hours of sleep at least four nights a week					
I exercise to the point of perspiration at least twice a week					
I take fewer than five alcoholic drinks a week					
I am the appropriate weight for my height					
I drink fewer than two cups of coffee (or tea or cola) a day					
I have one or more friends to confide in about personal matters					
I am generally in good health					
I am able to speak openly about my feelings when angry or worried					
I do something for fun at least once a week					
I always recognise stress symptoms					
I take quiet time for myself during the day					
I spend less than an hour each day travelling to and from work					
I never race through a day					
I never feel disorganised and out of control					
I am able to organise my time effectively					
SUBTOTAL minus 15 =					**TOTAL**

To get your score, add up the figures, then subtract 15. Any number over 7 indicates a vulnerability to stress. You are seriously vulnerable if your score is between 20 and 45, and extremely vulnerable if your score is over 45 and your health and wellbeing are in serious danger.

What Makes You Stressed?

There are two things that create stress:

1. not having something you want; and
2. having something you don't want.

Not having something you want

Do you want something so much that it's dominating your thoughts, but you can't have it? That house, car, holiday? Working fewer hours, that job, the perfect lover? Peace and quiet or simple happiness would do! Focusing on what you haven't got creates stress. Not only does it create stress, but it also creates anxiety, anger, sorrow, frustration, bitterness, loneliness, shame and guilt. Your mind is like a demented honeybee unable to find nectar on a flower. The angry-bee buzz is conducted through your obsessing, planning and fervour. But, *when* you get what you want, *then* you'll stop being stressed.

Having something you don't want

Or do you have something you don't want: debts, a bad relationship, too much responsibility, a rotten job? It's the same as not having what you *do* want.

Negative thoughts stir up your emotions like a stick stirring up a muddy pond. Here is proof of that. If you think about something you have but don't want – let's assume debts are the problem – for one minute, make yourself believe you have won the top lottery prize. Spend the minute planning how you would pay off your debts and imagine going to each debtor with the cash and squaring your outstanding payments. Can you feel the release and calm within your body where your emotions lie? Or it may be that you are in ill health. Again, spend a minute imaging yourself as fit and healthy. Can you see the difference?

Calming Stress

As you feel your stress return because you haven't got what you want, can you say to yourself, for the moment, this is as good as it gets? Can you accept all that you have right now? Assume you are totally content with what you've got and that you will cease to berate yourself because you have been unable to achieve great heights, then can you sense the settling within yourself? Longing for something you can't get in this moment will only engender more longing. Right now, do you need that disturbance or can you accept it?

A technique to help combat stress follows, which can be done anywhere and any time. It is a way to take a couple of minutes, relax and gain a little perspective.

Sit or lie down comfortably. Let your thoughts come and go for a minute. You will sense the different feelings that your thoughts engender. Now, turn your racing thoughts into a calm and still lake. Watch the lake and visualise it as quiet and placid as a mirror. You know that in the deep waters your emotions are stored. But for the moment you feel the calmness of the surface. If your mind starts to race, simply witness it as a third party without judgement.

Notice how your feelings become calm and your stomach relaxes. As fear rises from the surface, let it float away on the surface of the lake until it becomes calm once more. Feel the beauty of the lake's surface. Feel the stillness in your soul.

This technique can be carried out any time. It need be only a few minutes long. It is a little sanctuary that you can dive into on tap. It is not meant to be an in-depth meditation but a tool to develop that will give you a bolthole in the middle of the day, when you are sitting on the Tube or the loo, when you have taken a break from a stressful meeting. It's one of those things that get better as you practise them.

Some Stress-busting Tips

- Do some exercise that makes you sweat; the endorphins you release will make you feel much more relaxed.
- Take up some yoga and let it smooth your ruffled feathers.
- Drink green tea.
- Rub lavender oil on to your temples.
- Watch a comedy.
- Prepare your bathroom: light some candles, put rose oil in the water and lock the door.
- Listen to your favourite music.
- Spend time with a fluffy animal that you can hug.
- The most important one: move into the Stillness and feel the moment.

I Have to Go to Work

'Nothing is really work unless you would rather be doing something else.'

James M Barrie, author

You've just got back from a great holiday and – oh, no! – you've got to go back to work on Monday. You'd pushed to one side those usual Monday-morning blues and had forgotten the feelings of dismay and desolation you usually face come the beginning of the week. Perhaps you have obsessed all holiday on what union uprising you will be instigating to get rid of your manager, who's made your life hell for the last year. Or maybe you run your own business and you can't wait to get back to make sure the whole company hasn't collapsed without you.

Whatever your perspective, there's no doubt that going to work takes up a huge amount of time and for some people work is everything. Many people put work into a chunk of their day, which means: go; do what I'm supposed to do to make money; leave; start living. While they're there they 'put life on hold', which means they pick up life when they leave. And, because the rest of their day revolves around getting dressed, going, coming back and resting, it means that the whole week is taken up with work and 'life' happens at the weekend. This numbing and deadening experience is not because of the job we do: it's because we are not in the moment.

Some people *are* able to get the Beach Life feeling at work. Do you instantly get a vision of bearded and beaded men and women wearing kaftans and sandals? People who enjoy simple lives, perhaps? Monks working in peace and harmony? Or a kibbutz, perhaps, within a communal regime? We often think that in order to enjoy work we have to *give up* something. Some people are convinced that the only way to be happy is to give up *everything* and go and run a beach bar in Greece. This is a fantasy, because, when you get to the beach in Greece, you have taken yourself with you, along with the very attitudes that sum up the inability to feel fulfilled regardless of the work you do. However, it is possible to go to work and enjoy yourself, regardless of your job.

Before we have a look at that, let's not be under any false impression: the organisation you work for may not be a good place to be to get that Beach Life feeling. You may be in a company that puts productivity above the wellbeing of the people who work there, and that can be soul-destroying. If this is your workplace and you feel there's no opportunity to create an expressive environment from which to flourish, then look for another job.

But hold up and see if you can incorporate some of the principles outlined below into your working day, which will help you make a more informed decision. Because, if you can't get satisfaction from work, it's worth eliminating a few things first to establish what isn't effective, and one of them is: how happy are you regardless of where you work? As in relationships, if you feel that your job isn't working for you, it's worth stepping back and identifying whether your unhappiness is due to the job or is within you. There is no point in taking the same state of mind into the next job.

Essentially, we all need to work. As long as people have been on Earth, work has been done. What the work is is irrelevant but what it symbolises is fourfold.

1. The opportunity to fulfil personal growth and potential which gives your work meaning.
2. The opportunity to fulfil your financial obligations and pay your way in the world.
3. To be part of an opportunity to create something with others that helps to bind you together.
4. To make a contribution to a world community.

It is very rare to meet someone who doesn't need to work who is at peace. Work is a natural part of our growth, contributing to our fulfilment and contentment. It enables us to feel that we're making a difference, and that feeds our esteem. It's important that we feel useful in our community. This is why so many people who don't go into a structured workplace seek volunteer jobs or community posts. It gives a feeling of adequacy and accomplishment.

Money

'My problem lies in reconciling my gross habits with my net income.'

Errol Flynn

You need money to live but you don't need lots to be happy. If you have enough to pay your bills and live simply, lots of extra money does not make you any happier. What makes you unhappy, though, is wishing and yearning for lots of things you don't have. If this is you, and you look for work to fund the extras that you wish and yearn for, how much do you compromise yourself in order to fulfil your material dreams?

Work isn't Life

But work isn't life! Work is what we do that sits on top of life. Real life sits underneath work and we get so caught up in work, money and competing with everyone else that we forget what's really important. Yes, we want our work to be fulfilling and we may as well try to make it so, because we spend a long time there; but it doesn't rule our happiness. Anyone can do their job and feel happy. If we are pursuing the perfect job to make us happy, we are idealising work as the thing to make us feel blissful.

There are two separate things: personal bliss and work fulfilment. One doesn't rely on the other to come true. If you have had the glimpse of the Stillness, you'll know that the shard of light that comes through for that moment was reality. The stuff, like work, is that: just stuff, not reality.

Allowing Your Creativity to Blossom

As you expand your conscious capacity, you will be allowing your creativity to blossom. Continuous expansion increases your capacity to open up to ideas you never thought of previously, as your boundaries for innovation increase. Moving into the moment is like an archer pulling back the bowstring. The more you move into the moment, the more your bowstring will be pulled back. The speed and direction of the arrow will become more targeted and this will reflect in all your activities, not just the workplace.

Your ability to concentrate will increase if for no other reason than that you are becoming more still and less harried. Your mind will become clearer, and this allows for more accomplished decisions. You may feel as though your intelligence has increased but bringing your attention into the Stillness only demarcates what you already possess.

Focusing the Mind

If you have watched a butterfly, you will have seen it flying from one flower to another: it appears to be flitting, but, when it finds the flower with the nectar, it settles down. This is how your mind works. It simply needs a reason to settle. It will not settle for the flower without any nectar: it will keep moving until it finds its perfect resting place – the Stillness.

There is a lot of mental energy used up when your mind is jumping around. If you are constantly mind racing you are draining your reserves of mental energy. If your mind is focused because you are living more and more in the moment, you will be conserving mental energy that can be put to better use in a more creative way.

Strengthening the Mind

Practising the Stillness will redirect your focus and strengthen your mind. A strong mind will have a positive effect on the whole nervous system and the physical body. This will increase your energy levels. This increased energy is your life energy, as in powerful thinking, enhanced clarity and increased creativity. You will be drawing this extra energy through your own natural resources and your bowstring will be pulled back long and strong, causing the arrow, or action, to be accurate and fast.

Bringing it to Work

The resources for focusing and strengthening the mind are limitless. Drawing energy from your own field of consciousness is unending. You will find changes in the way you approach work, whether seeing it in a wholly different way, enjoying it more, requesting better conditions or deciding to leave it altogether.

It is possible to move into the Stillness in your working day and be quite focused on your job. Being in the moment does not mean not being attentive in what you do: it means being completely attentive to what you do and your mind is definitely 'on the job'.

As far as planning ahead goes, you will find yourself planning as before but not being driven by results. Instead of focusing on the desired outcome next week or next month, you will be more involved in doing the necessary footwork, today, to get the job done. You will find yourself planning but not projecting and this will encourage a lot more productivity, which will in turn open new doors to find the work that perfectly fits into your 'Life's a Beach' plan.

I've Got Too Many Dramas

'No drama, however great, is entirely independent of the stage on which it is given.'

George P Baker, playwright

It isn't until you step on to that plane, the doors are sealed and you start to move away from the passenger terminal that you begin to feel that you are leaving the overload behind. Aaahhh, it's too good to be true: nothing to worry about for two whole weeks. Utter bliss. You take a big breath and relax. You can leave all your dramas behind you and get on with being happy. This is what you've worked hard for all year. This is what you have dreamed about and, finally, you are here.

But, maybe not. Maybe you're going to miss all the normal dramas of your life. Being without your dramas can feel as if the rug's been pulled away from under you. Then again, you could keep in touch with what's going on by text so you're not missing out! Perhaps you've taken the dramas with you and now you can create mayhem while you're away. If that is you, have you ever been described as a drama king or queen (DKQ)?

A DKQ is someone who is easily excitable with a penchant for creating a commotion. Anyone can be a DKQ and you can make a drama out of anything. DKQs tend to want to be the centre of attention in any group and will do anything to get it. They create life-or-death situations when they aren't warranted, just to gain attention. They become chronic liars because they have to make up stories to substantiate the drama. They don't think they are lying but simply telling the story the way they see it. A DKQ has little capacity for empathy and sharing with others. If a friend or partner cannot provide the buzz they need on which to thrive, they are abandoned.

Do you see any of these traits in yourself? You may have something of the DKQ in you – most people do – and you recognise the stress it causes you. As you move into the Stillness you will sense a feeling of roundedness and grounding that will be so different from leading

54

the life of drama that you're so used to. It may take a little time to get used to these new feelings.

We did a short exercise earlier in the section 'The Journey There' with a kitchen work surface. Let's do that now. Imagine that kitchen worktop again, this time full of all your dramas. Now bring your hands together as if in prayer. Move them down on to the kitchen counter and then spread them outwards creating a space. As you do this, recognise that you are moving your dramas aside, just for this moment, and sense getting to the levelness below. Hold your hands there and feel the bliss of having no dramas in this moment.

Become aware of the space around you. Listen for the sound of life. Smell the scent of your environment. Be fully in tune with your senses. Feel the bliss of life. Submit yourself to the moment. Allow all to be as it is.

Stilling Your Life Drama

Your Life Drama is the spin cycle on a washing machine and the spinning action generates stress. All your dramas are circling in the tub. As more adrenalin is produced through your dramas, the idea of switching the machine off becomes less and less a reality and peace seems so far away. Being away from home means being away from all the life dramas and their stresses. That is one of the most blissful things about being on holiday: you don't have to deal with your own and others' palavers and you can take a mental break. Oh, the peace! It really is a joy. How is it possible to get that peace back home?

Maybe you feel alive only when you have a drama. Does your self-esteem rise when you get through it, 'stronger than before'? Yes, there are ways you can prepare yourself for action at any time by being vigilant, on guard and generally stressed – but this will keep you stuck in the spin cycle.

Life Drama is when you see life as a series of good and bad events. It's the black-or-white thinking that polarises events into a series of crises. The outcome of the crises is usually either: (a) just emerged unscathed or (b) waded in and saved the day. You may be filtering your experiences through a lens of polarity: good luck/bad luck, black/white, success/failure.

Your Life Drama has its place: it protects you from your own sorrow, allowing you to focus on others' lives or the catastrophe that will engulf you next week. But maybe you are paying a great price by keeping yourself stuck in your Life Drama and therefore stuck in the spin cycle. The spinning doesn't allow you to relax and feel your true legacy – true bliss. When you begin to see all Life Drama as neutral, you will understand that you have created your own perspective on situations based on your own lens filter.

Try seeing all the dramas in your life as scenes in a TV comedy drama. As you play them through your mind, as if you were watching the programme, you will begin to grasp the neutrality of these and all dramas that take place. Bring your focus into the moment and feel the space that appears between you and your Life Drama. Sense the bliss that pervades you; feel the silence that surrounds you. See the drama as another entity.

But how can I when I have debts to pay? kids in trouble? or about to lose my job? Then you do what you can do right now: restructure your debts, talk to your child, look for another job – and then you let go of the future. This isn't saying that you have no dramas, and this isn't about sorting everything out so you can then be happy: this is about finding the Stillness underneath your problems. Everyone has life dramas and always will.

Wear the World as a Loose Garment

Isn't this what you do when you're on holiday? You wear loose clothes that make you feel more comfortable? This is how to wear the world. You wear the drama that surrounds you like a loose garment. Your Life Drama is not you and it doesn't define you. You have a choice as to whether you wish to be a part of it. It doesn't mean you are not involved. As you practise coming into the Stillness, your sense of humour will grow. The absurdity of Life Drama can seem funny and you will gain a new perspective. In fact, you will find that the excitement of being a DKQ starts to wear off as giving life's dramas lots of attention distracts you from your Beach Life.

I'm Too Miserable

'Life is full of misery, loneliness and suffering – and it's all over much too soon.'

Woody Allen

Do you ever feel that you can't reach that Beach Life place because you are depressed? It may not be a full-blown depression that requires a consultation with your GP, a trip to the couch doctor and a course of antidepressants, but it could be a low-level, sitting-just-below-the-surface-and-hovering-around-unnecessarily type of depression.

Low-level melancholy is extremely common. It feels like a light cloud swirling around and keeping stuff pressed down. While it keeps down the negative feelings, it also keeps down the positive feelings. It's not exclusive. It is a greyness that pervades most of your life, not in a way that will make you feel despair but more a feeling of dissatisfaction with your lot. Just not happy. Want something else but not sure what. 'Is this it? Do I have everything I need to be happy? Then why am I not happy?'

Confronting high-level, chronic (more than three months ongoing) depression is not what this book is about. If you feel you need to confront chronic depression, then my book *Beat Depression and Reclaim Your Life* (Virgin Books, 2004) is the book to do that.

This book is about acceptance. By accepting what is you will come towards a state of peace more quickly than if you fight it. Fighting low-level depression is like trying to run out of quicksand: the more you move, the more you sink. By accepting what is, in this moment, you will come through your dejection intact and integral.

Accepting what is – it can feel like a tall order. Does that mean you sit with your feelings even if they are really, really uncomfortable? Yes, it does to a certain extent. Sitting with your feelings is acceptance of what is. What other choice do you have? Your other choice is to keep running from your discomfort and this is what you have probably been doing all your life, but it has not fulfilled you. We are used to our society telling us that we should 'pull our socks up', and not to 'wallow in our misery' and other such orders that equate to ignoring our feelings. But these actions have not brought you the peace and bliss that you crave. So, what is your alternative? It is to accept your discomfort and let the feelings come.

What is this discomfort? This discomfort is a blend of hidden pain and anger. Hidden pain and anger are two ends of a seesaw. One does not exist without the other. Have you ever cried 'tears of frustration'? This is the classic moment when pain and anger come together. You may cry when you feel angry; conversely, you may feel angry when you're in pain. They go together, hand in hand. Do you think this is nonsense and you feel neither? Here is a checklist for hidden pain/anger:

- chronic pain in the neck or jaw;
- sarcasm;
- ironic humour;
- boredom, apathy, uninterest, can't be bothered;
- nightmares;
- smiling when you don't want to;
- controlling your voice;
- grinding your teeth at night;
- becoming irritated at irrelevant things;
- body tics or spasmodic movements that you are unaware of;
- stomach ulcers;
- constant cheerfulness and grin-and-bear-it attitude;
- refusing eye contact;
- clenching a thumb in a fist;
- overpoliteness;
- not sleeping, or sleeping too much;
- frustration at everything around you;
- a feeling that life's not good enough.

If you have ticked three, then you probably have hidden pain/anger.

Hidden pain/anger keeps down your warm feelings of joy and delight. Denying your hidden pain/anger helps those feelings to grow into frustration and despair. You can find ways of gently acknowledging your hidden pain/anger and allowing it to release itself, liberating you from its burden.

Releasing Hidden Pain

Hidden pain can grow into a dangerous monster if left unattended and this can fan the flames of destruction. Hidden pain will metamorphose into reckless anger, which can damage relationships through its mindless lash. Left to its own devices, pain can grow and multiply, taking what was once a manageable situation and turning it into a vehicle of destruction. It defends itself with anger. Whether this is low-level anger or high-energy-rage, all-out-explosion anger depends on each individual, but the bottom line is that hidden anger stems from hidden pain.

Where does this pain come from? In this moment, is it important? Most people hold a residue of pain from past life losses. Society teaches you to ignore these feelings of loss: 'Pull your socks up or stop moping about.' This will not coax you into the natural process of grieving each time you lose something but the pain doesn't go away: it simply hides under a rock.

Dissolving your Pain

To dissolve your pain you need to allow the energy of the pain to be released by being in the moment. You observe the pain in your body: feel its presence, its shape and its source. Don't identify with it because you are not your pain. Instead, become the observer of it. Watch it as if you were watching a fountain. As each drop of water is released, so *you* are released. Let the tears come because they will heal you.

Now you have the tool to sweep your rocks for pockets of hidden sadness and shine the light on them, bringing them out into the sunshine. If settling into the Stillness brings pain, you are simply shining a healing light into the dark side of your soul. Do not be afraid: the pain passes. You will never, ever be handed more than you can handle.

When you have practised this once, you have accepted some control over your feelings. You no longer need to fear them and you will realise that the fear of trapped pain is greater than the pain itself. You will not lose control by being in tune with these feelings; you will, in fact, be more in control.

Clearing your hidden pain won't take as long as you think, for it is the fear of the pain that is much, much more powerful than the pain itself. The pain will last a relatively short time compared with how long it has been hiding. As you let out your tears, remember, tears are the coins of healing. Accept the pain in the Stillness. Don't judge it; simply observe it.

As you accept and release your pain in the Stillness, these things will take place:

- your anxiety will decrease;
- you will feel calmer;
- you will feel clearer;
- you will feel more in control;
- you will feel more and more bliss;
- you will laugh more;
- you will have that Beach Life moment.

Releasing Hidden Anger

As you release your hidden pain you will recover your hidden anger. Hidden pain and hidden anger are brothers-in-arms. They help, support and encourage each other. If there is plenty of one there is plenty of the other. They work in tandem: one is out while the other stays hidden. But, like the woman and man in the cuckoo clock, when one goes back in, the other comes out.

It's time to acknowledge your hidden anger and sort it out so it doesn't hold you back any more. This is a two-pronged approach: (1) working through the emotions and (2) moving yourself into the Stillness.

Working through the emotions

What is lying underneath your frustration and fed-up-ness? Take an hour aside for yourself and sit somewhere quiet and safe. Begin to write about what angers you. Make a list of at least ten things. You will start to see a common theme. Whatever your common theme is, allow yourself to indulge in the feelings that accompany your list. The ten things on your list will guide you to exactly what is at the centre of your anger. Don't be alarmed when you discover it's not what you thought it would be – it never is.

Now that you know what it is, take action to dispel the anger: thump the pillow, run it out, throw rocks in the sea, scream your head off or do something that satisfies the energy you feel. Release it but contain your fear that you will go out of control – you won't. Your mind will release only what you can deal with at that moment. Don't be afraid of your anger because it is very powerful. Use it for your good. Move it into determination, resolve and purpose. Make it work for you to bring about change.

Anger, when properly managed, can move mountains. It can take you from a place of insecurity, fear, low self-esteem and chronic depression to feeling strong, capable, alive and, most importantly, present. When you fully mobilise your anger in an appropriate and constructive way you begin to feel safe in the world.

Moving yourself into the Stillness

If you come into the Stillness and feel agitated, this is probably anger. Allow the disturbance to come to the surface. Accept it as it is. Embrace it because it is indicating to you that somewhere changes need to be made. But these changes do not need to be a knee-jerk reaction.

Once you have accepted the validity of your anger, you can use it to address matters with others. Addressing matters with others when appropriate will lessen your anger. Rage is born through unaddressed anger. If you acknowledge and release your anger, you will quieten your soul.

When you feel the anger, you may notice that it's being pushed out by a gush of pain. Anger is usually fronting pain. Allow the pain to rise with the anger. Acknowledge them both, address your matters and allow them to leave. By staying in the Stillness you will gain the impetus you need to clear your backlog of anger, which will liberate you in so many ways.

As you feel the healing, you will:

- feel stronger;
- feel protected;
- trust yourself more;
- feel more trusting in the world;
- move from fear to trust;
- move from anxiety to reassurance.

A promise

As you release your hidden pain/anger, you will begin to notice some profound changes taking place. Your view of life will alter. Whereas life may have seemed like a huge mountain to climb or race to run, you will now see it as a soft, enlightening place to be; whereas life was something to 'get through', now you see it as something to 'get from'. Healing your hidden pain/anger is 'restorative', balancing and calming.

People have less and less effect on you. Now you are no longer enmeshed in your pain and anger and you have found space for objectivity. You don't feel threatened by others any more. You can fill yourself up through the bliss consciousness that comes from within and look for approval in others much less. This in turn cultivates self-trust and authority.

You will giggle through life. What you once thought to be the end of the world will start to feel light and funny. You will come to realise that it was perhaps *you* who allowed 'stuff' to come into you and have a negative effect on you.

One Amazing Thing

There is one amazing thing that you can do that will change the way you feel within hours.

Get a photograph of you as a child. Or think of a time when you were young and see where you were and what you looked like in your mind's eye. When you feel miserable, close your eyes so that you can see yourself as a child. Pay attention to your feelings; they may be turbulent and vigorous.

Go up to up to the child and soothe him/her in a way that feels good. Talk to him/her as you are now. Soothe the child in the same way as you would soothe any child. Tell him/her that everything is going to be OK and explain that these feelings will pass.

It is a simple exercise and this is all you have to do to feel immediate results. Within fifteen minutes you will notice a difference and, if you practise frequently, you will find comfort on a regular basis. You may feel miserable because you're not in tune with yourself. This technique (adapted from *Beat Depression and Reclaim Your Life*) cuts through all your defences like a hot knife through butter.

If you post notes around your house to *remind* yourself to do this whenever you need to, you will remember to do it more often. If you live with others and would be embarrassed by this exercise, then write something in code, draw a picture or put it where only you can see it. The more often you do it, the better you will feel. You will feel soothed and sometimes that's all you need to pick yourself up.

I've Got Too Many Problems

'The robbed that smiles, steals something from the thief.'

William Shakespeare, *Othello*

Being away from home can seem like a wonderful escape from 'reality' and all those life 'problems'. Just imagine plunging into far-flung places where other people can't get hold of you and, for a few days, real life is another existence. Even though you know you have to face your stresses on your return, for that fixed chunk of time you are free from worry.

But – and here it comes, the big 'but' – as soon as you get home and the holiday blues set in, you find yourself full of life problems again. The debts, your job, your parents . . . They crowd in on you and, frankly, leave no time for any peace. Before you know it you're spinning again and find yourself turning to drinking, spending money you don't have in order to cope or slumping into a depression because it's too much to cope with. How do you challenge all of these problems and minimise their effect on you? How can you be happy with all these problems?

Everybody has problems. But the control that problems have over you is down to you and how you see them. There is no point in trying to end all your problems believing that this will make you happy, because, no matter how many problems you have, you will always find more. As soon as one problem is sorted, you will have another, if this is how you have lived your life until now. This is a modern Western endemic attitude and you are not alone.

What matters is how you see your life *underneath* your problems. There are your *life problems* and there is your *life*. Your life problems can obscure your life with unnecessary clutter. Take this moment to decide what problems you have right now. Not what problems you have tomorrow, later today or in an hour's time. No, the problems you have *right now*. As you think about those problems, decide whether they are problems that you have right now or are a fantasy of what *might* happen if your fears come true.

As you move into the moment, you will see that, right now, you have no problems and you will feel the astonishing clarity of this moment. You may say, 'Yes, but my problems are still here.' Yes, but where? Unless you are undergoing an immediate emergency (and you would not be reading this if you were), then right in this moment you have no problems. You may have circumstances that need attending to – we all do – but right now you have no problems.

Life isn't a series of problems to be overcome. Living life with lots of problems causes chronic pain and stress. When you go on holiday you leave behind the numbing mind racing that accompanies a life of problems. You spontaneously move into the moment because you have made a conscious decision to 'leave your worries behind'. Not only do you worry less but you also may have that wondrous moment when you have entered a majestic temple or climbed a sheer rock and you have been in awe at the beauty of that point in time. You are captivated by the purity of that moment, which is neither the past nor the future. Indeed, it is the purity of the Stillness and you are experiencing its sacredness.

The realisation of the moment is profound. As you increasingly move into the moment you will create a bigger space between your problems, and the associated stress will decrease. You will reach a point where your problems become less significant and your capacity for managing them becomes greater. As you strengthen your ability to move into the Stillness, you will find yourself naturally progressing into it more and more.

Just as you 'let go' of your problems while you are on holiday, so you will begin to let go of your problems in everyday life. This doesn't mean you ignore your problems: it means that you don't see your problems as your whole life. You will come to see your problems as circumstances to be managed. As you assess your problems, decide what you can control and what you can't. Can you make a call, write a letter or talk to someone? If so then you have a choice to take action. If you can't do anything about your problems, let them go.

ENJOYING THE RIDE: BEING THERE

Kick back, relax and enjoy the ride! Just being there is good enough because it takes you away from the entanglement of a nine-to-five existence. Holidays give us the opportunity to be actively lazy, to abandon duty and responsibility and to romp in personal playtime. The following pieces encompass playtime and suggest ways to bend the rules and bring the same ideas back home.

Sun, Sea, Sand, Sangria and Sex

'Come, woo me, woo me; for now I am in holiday humour and like enough to consent.'

William Shakespeare, *As You Like It*

You don't need the science to know when your body feels good, you feel good. There are enough headlines screaming out the messages:

MODERATE EXERCISE YIELDS BIG BENEFITS

HAPPINESS IS A WARM SUN

HAVE THAT HOLIDAY GLOW? MUST BE THE EXTRA SEX

FOOD FOR THOUGHT BOOSTS YOUR MOOD

Life's a beach

First There's the Sun

It's all there on holiday. Even on a cold holiday you tend to see a lot more of the sun than you would do at home for the simple reason that you're more likely to be outside. Soaking up the rays, even if it's cold outside, gives a definite mood boost. Even if you live in a warm climate, you are caught up in a daily routine that often leaves no time for outdoor enjoyment.

And, while you're outdoors, you're not indoors! Indoors means phones, TVs, computers, lists, games consoles, fax machines and personal handheld computers. And, if you're very lucky, your holiday destination won't have any signal for your mobile phones. Phew!

Then There's the Sea

Whether you're trekking over hills, skiing, camping in the outdoors, sailing in dodgy conditions or swimming in some glorious warm sea, you are active. Activities that you do on holiday have a lot to do with how good you feel. It's not just being outdoors but also about being physically energetic. Burning off the calories while cramming your body with the feel-good endorphins, giving you a sparkle that is hard to find at home.

And then There's the Sand

Being outside means you are with nature. And, as corny as that may sound, being with nature has a profound effect on your emotional wellbeing. When you explore the local geography of your holiday destination, you recover a sense of awe and wonder that you'd forgotten you had. Do you remember seeing a huge outdoor plant that you'd only seen in an indoor pot back home? Wasn't it weird and wonderful? Those delicious moments bring you right into the moment, help you forget about your mental chatter and touch the childlike part of you.

The difference in the surroundings can bring a sharp focus. For example, your sense of smell may be sharper as you breathe in the scent of the sea or wet trees. Maybe some mist gives a magical appearance to the environs, adding a little mystery that reminds us that we don't know everything and we are a small part of a huge ecosystem.

Returning to nature can help you get a perspective on your life back home. The problems you left behind seem insignificant compared with the pulsating life that now surrounds you and it was in that unfamiliar environment that you recognised how out of step with nature you had become.

Get on your bike!

It's not hard to get that outdoor feeling back home. Ditch the car and get on your bike. Failing that, get a dog or an allotment. Getting outdoors helps boost the feel-good factor as well as keeping you fit. Never mind if it's cold outside – it's also nourishing outside. Keeping that holiday feeling going isn't as hard as you think.

And Now the Sangria

Oh – the local food and drink. When will it end? Let's hope never! Sliding into the café on the beach and eating the local food is such a joy. And the local wine – don't you just love it?

Eating new foods is as much a part of the holiday as sightseeing. It's such a delight to eat food that's unfamiliar. Even familiar foods taste better on holiday. Similarly, cooking your own meals is a treat compared with back home. The one thing that is striking is what you *don't* eat when you're away: snacks such as crisps, chocolate and sweets, 'hoovering up' the kids' leftovers or indulging in the office round of cakes. Your meals tend to be more regular and you leave out the little high fat/salt/sugar 'extras' that creep in at home.

Shopping for food is so much more relaxing than at your local supermarket back home. The smells, sounds and tastes of the local market abound. Because we buy unusual things we tend to buy more fresh foods as well as fewer processed foods. Foods even sound better:

'peaches' – the word sounds juicy and sun-kissed. You can imagine the fruit being picked from the tree a few hours before. And it probably was. Eating a local melon tastes so much better than the one you can buy at your local supermarket back home, even though it's the same fruit. And it's usually cheaper, which makes it seem all the more fun.

It's not that you don't want to indulge in good food back home: it's just that it seems there's never as much time to shop and cook as there is when you're away. Buying, preparing and eating food can be an amazingly sensual treat. Consider how you eat at home and how you eat on holiday. Did you ever eat in front of the telly, throw a pizza in the oven or grab a sandwich on the run on holiday? Probably not. As you move into the Stillness, you will notice that, in preparing and eating food, there is a synchronicity between being in the moment and eating. Our relationship with food is a sensory indulgence that is best enjoyed slowly and without distractions.

And Finally the Sex

After all that activity, your body glows and gets you in the mood . . .

Good sex can only boost your mental, physical and emotional wellbeing. It's free, it's fun and it makes you happy. Forget your beach burnout when you can burn two hundred calories in thirty minutes of great sex. This in itself leads to better flexibility and strength. So much for the torture of the yoga class!

Sexual arousal and climax release endorphins, which reduce stress levels. It helps you sleep, boosts your immune system and relieves depression, and increased intimacy leads to increased self-esteem. Great sex increases the desire for more, and more sex increases vibrancy and creativity. So, what better way to get your exercise than to hit the sack?

When you get back home, instead of signing up for another year of a hit-or-miss attendance at the local gym, spice up your sex life and get all the great benefits without having to leave the house.

Blowing in the Wind

'So I said to the gym instructor, "Can you teach me to do the splits?" He said, "How flexible are you?" I said, "I can't make Tuesdays." '

Tim Vine, comedian

Have you noticed that when you're on holiday everything seems to have a sheen to it? There is luminosity to life that isn't apparent back home. It's as if this other town, city or country holds a magic that bathes you in weightlessness and leaves you feeling more radiant. The long chains of responsibility, stress and time chasing have vanished and the benumbing anchors are no longer holding you down. You feel free and happy, and find yourself doing what you want to do and not being at the beck and call of everyone else's requirements. The absence of pressure leaves a vacuum into which lots of goodies pour, leaving you to float on a natural high.

At the hub of this delectable mood is a self-love that you are not always able to find when you are in the rough and tumble of your daily life. But you know what it feels like and you want to experience it all the time. When you are on holiday you have the benefit of time, and this is not always possible to maintain once you are back home. But you know that life is short and you want more of the good stuff.

By 'blowing in the wind' you can find more of this good stuff. What does this mean? It means to flow *with* life rather than struggle *against* it. It means to move *with* the wind rather than push *against* it. It means to enjoy the experience rather than try to find what's wrong with it – and yourself.

In order to accept life fully, you need to accept yourself fully, too. Accepting yourself fully leads to a peaceful mind. There is no point trying to force yourself to be happy with life when you're not happy with yourself. Self-acceptance is the hardest but most enlightening path to living a Beach Life. Here's a guide to what you can do to come to completely accept yourself.

71

Relinquishing the Need to be Perfect

'No one is perfect . . . that's why pencils have erasers.'

Anonymous

At some level we are all striving to be perfect because we think that, once we're perfect, we will be acceptable. We live in a world that positively embraces perfectionism. Simply look at the media and their interpretation of how we should live our lives. Everything looks perfect.

We may feel the need to be faultless in order to keep ourselves from our emotions. Perfectionism fosters a lack of sensation in the body because, when the small voice pipes up with 'Do you think we may be off track?' the big voice comes booming in with 'Don't be utterly ridiculous!' or some such command, which will whitewash any hesitation. Feeling numb is a great way of keeping us invulnerable, so we don't have to need anyone else's help or support. It keeps us safe from being intimate and we don't have to risk opening up to others.

In the quest for perfectionism, we have to put aside our human frailties and concentrate on being ideal. But, when we think about someone we adore, it's not their perfection we adore: it's their flaws we find so endearing. Flaws keep us striving and pushing and trying harder. They make us take risks and try again. They push us out of our comfort zone, where we tremble with anticipation. But all along we grow up each time we give up ways to keep ourselves looking perfect.

Indeed, perfection is not human. The price of staying perfect is huge. And paying this price can have devastating effects on your life: unhappy relationships, feelings of isolation, self-flagellation and piling on the shame. Is it worth it? It certainly doesn't give you that Beach Life you are looking for. Changing your *modus operandi* is frightening but the small price of change is negligible compared with the price of perfection, which is ruinous.

By bringing your awareness into the moment you will be instigating changes that will help you change your perfectionism and more easily accept yourself as someone who blows in the wind. The strength that you will gain from continually bringing your awareness into the Stillness will sustain you through all your changes and you will embrace your humanity much more easily. Living a more humble life helps you to connect with others and to recognise that, at some level, everyone is the same. It will help to diminish your ego, which drives you into the ground while demanding attention and accolade from the world. The strength you will gain will nourish you in a way that will make you need it less from others. Peculiarly, the very thing you strive for through perfectionism, which is acceptance, you will receive much more liberally through acknowledging your limits.

Embracing Your Mistakes

'The greatest mistake you can make in life is to be continually fearing you will make one.'

Elbert Hubbard, writer

Hey, we all make mistakes! But, it's part of our nature. Think of George W Bush – he makes plenty of mistakes. Here's a classic: 'We need an energy bill that encourages consumption' (New Jersey, September 2002).

But a mistake offers us an opportunity to grow. Do you beat yourself up when you get it wrong? Do you feel bad and ashamed for those mistakes you've made? By living in the moment you can embrace your mistakes by admitting them to yourself and learning from them. You will give yourself a break from self-shame and self-blame.

Start by admitting your mistakes to yourself and stop punishing yourself. Avoiding acknowledgement of your mistakes leads to a non-acceptance of yourself and then others. It takes a lot of negative energy to hide mistakes but admitting mistakes releases positive energy, which leaves you free to dwell in the present moment. A clean mind is a clean life and accepting your mistakes will help you to live in a 'clean house'.

By living cleanly you are fully acknowledging your humanity. You will become softer and less judging of others. You will learn to accept others' mistakes without harsh criticism. You will take time for perspective and you will relinquish the emotion attached to your mistakes.

Living Neutrally

'To a brave man, good and bad luck are like his left and right hand. He uses both.'

St Catherine of Sienna, Italy

There is a story about an old Chinese farmer who ploughed his field with his also very old horse. One day the horse escaped his harness and disappeared into the countryside. Everyone felt sorry for the old farmer because of his bad luck. And, as always, the farmer replied, 'Good luck? Bad luck? Who knows?' The following day the horse returned with a herd of wild horses from the savannah renowned for their strength and intelligence. This time the farmer's neighbours congratulated him on finding such a fantastic group of horses to help him attend his fields. The farmer replied, 'Good luck? Bad luck? Who knows?'

The following day the farmer's son was attempting to tame one of the horses when it reared up and kicked him in the back. The son was badly injured and had to lie down for some months. Everyone sympathised with the farmer on his misfortune and he replied, 'Good luck? Bad luck? Who knows?' The following day the farmer received a visit from an army recruiting officer who had come to recruit his son into the army. When the officer saw that his son was injured and unable to work he went away. His friends were thrilled by his good fortune, since as his son was spared the army. The farmer responded, 'Good luck? Bad luck? Who knows?'

When you are living neutrally you aren't placing any emphasis on the outcome of events. If something happens that may have once seemed to be bad luck, it doesn't worry you so much. If you have a great success at work, it doesn't affect you as much. The outcomes you experience don't please or displease you as much as they did before. You have more choice over your response but you are not as attached to the outcome as you once were.

By relinquishing the need to be perfect, embracing your mistakes and living neutrally, you are blowing in the wind. Like a tall palm tree, you are rooted in the earth and you are moving with the wind of life itself. You are not buffeted by the weather as you once were but you better handle what comes at you. Life events are often random and by understanding this you will not be so involved in the outcome and you will not construe it to be personal to you.

Interpretation of life will become more even because you are aware how much you create your own reality. You will see that you have choices in how to respond to life situations, even in the most severe situations. You will be more willing to trust yourself as you move deeply into the moment and sense your feelings. And, by allowing your feelings to be, to come and go, you will no longer feel like one of life's victims. You will have more fun, as if you were on holiday and not having to take the world as seriously as you once did.

Exploring the Beach

'He who wonders discovers that this in itself is wonder.'

M C Escher (1898–1972), Dutch artist

One of the best things about being away is exploring the local area. Walking through new landscapes, smelling the unusual smells and talking to the locals is a wonderful experience. It serves to remind us that our world back home is only a small part of the whole world and there is so much to explore, especially when everything feels sparkly and fresh. Does this part of your holiday grab you? The simple experience of another world? It takes you out of yourself and you forget your everyday life. It's the new experience that is so much fun.

You can liken this experience to a child's. Do you remember wandering outside when you were young and finding the garden a wondrous place? The smells and sights, the touch and feel – it felt new and mesmerising. What was so captivating was the dark area, the bits ready for exploration: the bushes and trees, dark musty sheds and shadowy spots where the compost heap sat. Exploring the shady areas was fun and you found the bugs and muddy bits more exciting than the open lawn. Rather like walking through the backstreets of a city where you can sense the real community life going on.

When you return home do you feel a little bit desolate because that's over for another year? Do you think you have to get your head down and back into the old routine until next year, when you get away again – and only then can you feel that good? Here's an interesting fact about spiders that may nudge you out of complacency. Did you know that the tensile strength of spider silk under normal laboratory conditions is about the same as steel, but five times as elastic? There are wonders of nature everywhere and those feelings of awe are still in you. You have only to tap into them to reawaken your wonder. Here are two ways to do it: the wonder of the Stillness and exploring your own world.

The Wonder of the Stillness

In the Stillness you use your senses totally. In the gaps between your thoughts you will become aware of the wonder of life. The smell, the touch, the colours and textures. Turn a circle and look all around you. Don't judge what you see but allow it all to be just as it is. Can you feel a lightness inside you? If you are sitting in your office, take 'a moment'. Just feel still and look around you. Is it a wild inundation of energy and colour? Most offices are. If you are at home, become still and sense your surroundings. Can you feel the vibration of your home through the shapes, colours and textures? If you are with children, sit with them in the moment. Are they not just balls of creativity and fun?

As you move into the stillness, you will awaken to your own

wonder. It's exciting. You have probably become desensitised to bright colours, loud noises, heavy smells and a river of fast-moving information. This has caused you to lose your natural awe and subdue your senses. As you spend more time in the moment, your anaesthetised senses will start to come to life. It won't take long for you to be amazed at your surroundings. It will feel as if a window has been cleaned. You may not hang on to the moment for long, but don't be dismayed. It took years for your filter to be smudged. Be patient.

These are the senses that you use on holiday while exploring the new locale. You are less stressed and you naturally allow your senses to guide you. Once you get home, perhaps your stress returns and you feel it's simply too indulgent to allow yourself that moment. You may keep yourself stressed through your mind racing, the constant shrill of thought going on in your mind as you relentlessly play out scenarios, the what-ifs and what-might-never-bes. These tactics numb you and your senses and the best way to tackle this epidemic behaviour is to say, *Stop*! ... and take this moment ... feel your lightness ... sense the wonder ...

Exploring Your Own World

The second gateway into wonder is to explore your own world – yourself – and look at ways of creating self-actualisation or a fulfilment of potential.

Self-actualisation is to be interested in solving problems, spontaneous in making decisions and taking action. It's to be creative, not just in practical tasks but also within the family, among friends and in social activities. People who have reached self-actualisation share certain characteristics such as having a strong support network but not necessarily a large one. They feel close to other people and have a strong moral value system. They are objective without prejudice and they focus their energy on one main task in life: their life's mission.

Working at fulfilling potential and becoming self-actualised generally comes down to three main areas: empathy, congruence and grace.

Life's a beach

1. Empathy
This is being able to relate to another's feelings and experiences without judgement or criticism or feeling them as your own. It means to recognise that everyone has their own path, and your path, or the way you see it, is not necessarily the right path for anyone else.

2. Congruence
This means when your inside and your outside match. This happens when you can be completely open and honest about your internal thoughts and feelings and it matches your external behaviour. You seem to others the way you seem to yourself. You have dropped any façade.

3. Grace
You live within a state of grace when you hold someone in a high regard without judging their actions, feeling or thoughts, even though you know their failings and dark side. And you have this attitude towards yourself at all times.

The steps in the table are what create a satisfying, 'living by the beach' life. These are the outcomes of self-actualisation.

What went before	Self-actualisation
Judgements and criticisms	High regard for others
To win or lose	No preferred outcome
Naïveté	Being highly developed
Arrogance	Humility
Defensiveness	Openness and honesty
Inflexibility	Allowing the flow of life
Anger	Allowing the pain of loss
Knowing everything	Opening the mind
Ignorance	Discovery

You don't need to work hard at being mediocre. It doesn't realise your potential. To do this, don't allow old habits to block your progress to self-actualisation. You will know what they are – we all do. As you hit an old habit, acknowledge it and let it go. Don't criticise yourself for having blocks. Simply note it and drop it. Don't spend time analysing it because, when you are in the Stillness, analysis is of little value. You may encounter thousands of blocks. Drop them one at a time, one day at a time. Working towards your potential this way will help to make all your dreams come true.

Blending in With the Locals

'If I've fooled the locals then I've done my job!'

Brion James, actor

Yep – by day three you've got the beads on, the shell flip-flops and one of those funny hats! As soon as the sunburn on your nose has cooled down you'll be blending in with the locals. It doesn't take long to mingle. As long as you don't try to get too involved in anyone else's business and give the game away with your dodgy accent, you'll soon be assumed to be a native.

Apart from the experience itself, have you ever felt how delicious it is to be anonymous? The very fact that you aren't local gives you a distinction that sets you slightly apart from the others. It's with this objectivity that you can become a witness to what's happening around you but, because of your separateness, you also feel the powerful presence within you.

It's such fun people watching. There's a whole culture, language and routine that we couldn't understand if we tried. But somehow it doesn't matter! Can you remember being in a local café and not understanding a word people spoke but loving the flair and passion that surrounded the words? The fact that you didn't understand what they were saying was neither here nor there and it didn't hold you back from having fun when the waiter came to clear your table with a flourish and a big smile. It's completely liberating.

How do you get this liberated feeling back home? You can stretch the gap between you and others and draw an imaginary moat around you by doing two things: extricating yourself and becoming transparent.

Extricating Yourself

Do you ever think that life is difficult, complex, exhausting and frustrating? Perhaps you are overly involved in other people's lives and it's time to extricate yourself. You may not even recognise that you do this – it's just a normal way of life. But if you go away and feel relieved because there's no politics to deal with, it may be because you are too involved in other people's affairs.

In case you're unsure, here's a guide to what you may do at home cross-referenced to what you may do on holiday.

What you do at home	What you do on holiday
You gossip about people you know.	You would never gossip, because the details of the locals' lives are of no interest to you.
You help others before they've asked for help.	You would help someone only if there was an emergency.
You assume you know what others are thinking about you.	You can't know what the locals are thinking about you because you don't speak their language and you can't read their minds.
You get involved in another couple's row.	You would never get involved because it would be none of your business.
You feel bad when someone tells you a heartrending story.	You may not understand all the background of the story due to language and cultural differences so you may not feel anything, just hear the words.

You try to make someone else happy.	You can't make a local happy – you just haven't got that sort of power. Besides, you're going home tomorrow so you can't fulfil any promises you might make.
You think you know where the other person should be in their life.	You can't make any judgements of the locals because you don't really understand everyone's position.
There's a certain way you'd like people to treat you.	You have no expectations of how the locals treat you – you just hope it's with respect and, if it isn't, you'll get out of there.
Feel responsible for another adult.	You can't feel responsible for a local person on holiday – where would you start?
You don't like the way others behave.	You don't really mind how others behave because it doesn't affect you.

Extricating yourself means stepping back. If you build a moat around yourself, you can step back into your castle, where you feel safe, warm, calm and still. You don't have to jump over your moat, over someone else's moat and into their castle. No, really, you don't. It's perfectly viable for you to conduct your life from the safety of your castle. When anyone tries to step over your moat you can simply wind up the drawbridge and talk through the window.

This goes against the grain of what is 'normal'. Getting involved in other people's lives is what we do, isn't it? Yes, it is, but how much of it feels good compared with how much of it we could do without. If you feel as if you want a little more of the anonymity you experience while on holiday, it's not hard to implement these ideas back home. By extricating yourself from being too involved in others' lives you will reduce your overall stress levels.

Becoming Transparent

Becoming transparent? What does that mean? Am I not already transparent enough, thanks very much?

By 'becoming transparent' we are talking about how to react to other people. This is a brilliant tactic to use when you're too caught up in how other people see you. Imagine yourself as being transparent when you're with other people. Imagine that their words are flowing right through you and out the other side. You don't let the words stick to you because there's nothing for them to stick to. You allow the words to move in and out of you without having any effect on you. You don't allow nuances, body language or signals to affect you. You allow them to travel somewhere else but not into you.

To visualise this, assume that you have two doors, one in the front and one in the back. If you feel uncomfortable or anxious or compromised about something someone has said or done, you have let them in your front door. All you have to do now is to open your back door and let them out. Allow things to flow through you, rather than get stuck in you. Allow the air to come in and make a clean sweep right through you, which refreshes your house for new experiences.

This is a powerful technique, especially if you're prone to allowing what others say to affect you. By allowing yourself to become transparent you are immediately neutralising any effect that other people have on you.

Happiness Versus Pleasure

'Happiness usually takes the form of us; pleasure of me.'

Anonymous

Pleasure, happiness – they are same thing, aren't they? They are both positive feelings and, if you feel good, then you feel good! We're conditioned to believe that pleasure and happiness go into one box. Or that, if we pursue pleasure, happiness automatically follows. You have to be living on another planet not to get caught up in the race 'to get as much pleasure out of life in order to find happiness'. There's a distinct difference between the two – in fact they are worlds apart but both crucial parts of our world.

Pleasure is something that gives you a buzz, amusement, delight, entertainment or a kick. It is an indulgence, a diversion, a thrill, a satisfaction or a joyride. It is achieving a goal, delivering a promise or manifesting dreams.

Happiness is connecting with yourself, it is being in the moment, it is needing nothing from the outer world. It is continuous and everlasting. It is the moment you recognise nothingness. It is a pure stillness. It is personal joy in its supremacy. It is unshakable.

Happiness and pleasure are parts of life but they fulfil very different roles. Pleasures come and go. They vary day to day. They are transitory and fleeting. When you eat a delicious meal you sink in its exquisite pleasure, soak up the flavours and feel so, so satisfied when you've finished. But then the pleasure's gone, over with, until you eat again. Happiness is inside you always, even if you can't feel it. It's the joy of being alive and nourishing your body through food promotes bliss and contentment. It's different. After a pleasurable meal you would say, 'That was fantastic'; nourishing the body with good food, you would say, 'I feel fantastic.'

If we are the ocean, the seat of our happiness lies in its depths. Here the still waters run deep. They are rich with life and purpose. The depth of the ocean is the home of your soul and your spirit. It is infinite and unbounded. It is where your pure potential lies. It is the source of pure joy and there is no restriction on how deep you wish to go. There is nothing to hold you back from being there. There is nothing controlling the deep part of the ocean – it is free.

Pleasure is at the surface of the ocean. It is the movement of the waves, and these waves come and go. There are high waves and low waves, excited waves and calm waves. The waves are momentary and transient. They move according to the external conditions. They never last long, but are fleeting. Movement creates waves but movement doesn't touch the deep, still waters.

You have both happiness and pleasure in life. But they are different and they don't rely on each other.

You can undertake pleasures without experiencing happiness. But pleasures without deep happiness are fleeting and, if you don't have the potential to return to the deep ocean of happiness time after time, you may need more and more pleasure in order to stimulate your satisfaction.

To illustrate this, let's take money. If you spend money and get that pleasurable 'high', you might feel empty once the pleasure has passed. Or if your pleasure is in a couple of glasses of wine at night, then you may have to rely on the alcohol to feel 'good'. There's nothing wrong with life's pleasures but when they are masking a sense of emptiness then you may need more and more pleasure so you don't get any gaps in between the pleasurable 'highs'.

Compulsively needing pleasure to sustain a form of satisfaction ultimately leads to unhappiness. Without a sense of deep joy, compulsive pleasures become a burden to the soul. Compulsive pleasures mean being unable to do without them in order to sustain life. Compulsively making money, drinking, shopping, having sex, eating food for the 'fix', etc. are the path to deep dissatisfaction. Relying on these compulsively leads to addiction and misery because you need more and more to continue feeling 'OK'.

But, if you are deeply happy, you enjoy your pleasures but don't *need* them to get the feel-good factor and it becomes a very different game. You enjoy them so much more when you don't *have* to have them to give you that warm contented feeling that comes from pure happiness. Feeling completely at ease with life itself and then going out for an exquisite meal or sampling some delicious wine is life in a different league – lying 20,000 leagues under the sea.

You can be happy without needing pleasure. You can feel peace and contentment without requiring other people or things to give you the buzz. Happiness bubbles up from deep waters and fulfils you with or without life's pleasures. You can feel as content eating a sandwich or eating a fabulous meal. You don't look for 'stuff' to give you a thrill because you are thrilled anyway. But you can thoroughly enjoy the pleasures of life when they come along. In fact, you enjoy them all the more. It's the icing on the cake.

In truth, you may find that some pleasures are better left alone because they detract from that gorgeous blissful experience. Intensive shopping, eating rich food or indulging in a bottle of good wine may distract you from the sensation of just being there because of the stress on the nervous system that challenges your ability to be still. Life's indulgences can bring your level of awareness up from the deep and get it flapping about on the waves in a boat. You might have to hang on until you descend once more into your quiet place.

The best approach is the holiday approach. When you go away you settle down away from the mind racing. While lazing on the beach you feel your stress decreasing and your thoughts diminishing. You might find that you enjoy life's pleasures so much more and wonder why food never tastes this good at home! This is where happiness and pleasure harmonise. You could be quite contented not moving from your deckchair but, if you eat something delicious, it's simply a treat.

And what's so liberating is that you don't need to change your house, car, job, lover or life to get that holiday feeling. When you are in a state of happiness, it's constant; it doesn't change according to your pleasure levels. If you lose sight of it, you don't need to spend a wedge of money to get it back. You simply refer to the access points of the Stillness and – hey presto! – you're back on track. Being on holiday gives you the 'mental break' to establish your access points and when you come home you can continue the experience and make it happen every day.

The more you experience the Stillness the more you will find that your reliance on pleasures to satisfy you will diminish. It will seem as if things have changed, and they will, because you don't struggle to maintain the pleasure ride as much, and this will reduce your stress levels. You won't need to control your outside world to the same extent because your compulsion to influence people and things will decrease. It's the universal truth that you can be happier with less.

Sitting in the Shade

'Concentrate all your thoughts upon the work at hand. The sun's rays do not burn until brought to a focus.'

Alexander Graham Bell (1847–1922), scientist and inventor

Phew, it's hot out there! You're inclined to go into the shade. No matter how much sun cream you've lathered over yourself, you concede and move into the shade because, no matter what happens, the sun won't catch you there. Once you've moved your sun lounger into the shady spot, you know you can relax, maybe doze off, because you're safe. If the sun moves around and hints at disturbing your shade, you can adjust your lounger so you're completely covered again. It's a great metaphor for life and it beautifully illustrates the way you can get yourself into the safe spot.

Honouring yourself is part of living that Beach Life. It's easy to stay out too long in the sun and allow yourself to get burned. Getting burned can range from feeling a little hot on top of the shoulders to full-blown sunstroke, when a spell in hospital is the only thing between you and death! Our tolerance of the sun differs and, by knowing yourself and your limits, you can make sure that you are out of harm's way.

When you stay out in the sun you are allowing yourself to be scorched and in life that amounts to being scorched by others. It's not a benign world and nasty things do happen to good people. You will read many transcripts and spiritual teachings on how you should be kind to others, help those less fortunate than yourself, cultivate forgiveness, etc. But, if you go too far down that line, you may leave yourself open to the effects of others' anger, rage and corruption. You can do without these consequences, because they add nothing to your life.

Staying in the sun is a temporary affair and it becomes unhealthy to remain in it too long. In the same way, embracing relationships or events that are unhealthy is harmful to us. There will always be people who want to take more than we're prepared to give. If we're not diligent, we may dishonour ourselves by accepting criticism, subtle put-downs, sarcasm or more extreme acts, such as physical aggression and emotional abuse. While the Bible says we should 'turn the other cheek' it also says that we should be wise and discerning. We must stand up for ourselves and not allow others to overstep our boundaries, otherwise we become resentful towards ourselves as well of others.

Setting Boundaries

When the sun begins to peep out between the leaves of the palm tree, you get up and move the sun lounger a few inches the other way. In the same way, do you update and reinstall your boundaries on a regular basis? It would be wise to do this, as it helps keep you safe and diminishes any long-term effects. Boundaries are imaginary lines that help you protect yourself both physically and emotionally. They protect you from others' actions and behaviours and stop them from hurting, distracting, annoying or frustrating you. Boundaries are limits you lay down which show how others can treat you. The table shows some illustrations of boundaries.

Healthy boundaries	**Unhealthy boundaries**
You are confident this person is safe to open up to. Leaving some time before sharing everything.	You tell them everything on the first meeting.
You allow a relationship to develop. You know the qualities you look for in another and you take time to look for those qualities in others.	You fall in love straightaway.
You do not play games about how you feel just to get sympathy.	You act as if falling apart so someone will look after you.

You give as much as you can afford.	You give more than you can to gain approval.
When someone asks for help, you take a moment to decide if you can assist them or not.	You fall head over heels with anyone who asks for your help because you feel grateful to be asked.
You notice when someone else is trying to help you in a way that's invasive.	You're oblivious of others who try to involve themselves too much in your life.
You make decisions based on whether it's good for you and not by asking another if they will be 'hurt' if you say 'no'.	You accept 'gifts' from others (food, sex, etc.) that don't make you feel good.
You listen to opinions but make decisions for yourself.	You allow others to control your life.

Once you have reset your boundaries things change. It's not that *you* have to change: it's your reference to others that changes. People treat you as you allow them to and they will treat you according to how your boundaries are. Strong boundaries are important for protecting your body, mind and spirit, and this action can jump your life into a higher level because you are taking control of your life rather than allowing others to manipulate you. It's one of the most important areas in defining your Beach Life because of the impact it will have.

Setting boundaries seems to be a very difficult area. Do you find yourself saying yes when you mean no? This is a very common theme but, if there's one thing to bear in mind, setting boundaries is not about getting other people to change: it's deciding what you will not tolerate any longer and then conveying this.

Here is a quick tip on setting boundaries. There are three parts to it:

1. 'When you do/say . . .'
2. 'I don't like it because . . .'
3. 'If you continue I will . . .'

Numbers 1 and 2 set the boundary by telling the other person what they do that is unacceptable, and why it is unacceptable. Number 3 is what you will do if they go over the line (and you don't need to say this out loud to the other person).

A simple example: 'When you complain about my ironing I don't like it because you don't appreciate that I'm putting myself out for you (and, if you continue, I won't do your ironing any more).'

It may take some practice but when you do it you will start feeling less guilty about putting yourself first. Over time you will honour yourself and your limits and, finally, you will set your boundaries without even thinking about it. You will notice that you honour others' boundaries more and you're more respectful towards them, even if they aren't that way to you.

There are many instances when you are met by unpleasant behaviour in which you aren't going to set boundaries verbally, but you simply don't want to be around the other person and you want to get out of the sun and into the shade. You need an aura or bubble around you more than a verbal exchange. You need to grow a 'thick skin' that protects you from the harsh rays at all times. While you can move your sun lounger with specific intent when you are sunbathing, it's different when you are wandering around the marketplace and the sun is on you and off you as you dip in and out of covered stalls. It's a characteristic you want, more than a technique.

Once you get the idea of setting boundaries, you won't ever need to state them out loud. You will emanate them. The invisible bubble around you will send a message to others that you are not to be messed with. Your lines will be felt by others and, if they are in their bubble, they will sense them. Your boundaries will be pushed by people who don't have their own. But it won't take much for you to be clear about where you stand. It may only take a smile or a gesture to demonstrate 'no'.

To explain this further, you may know people who will not allow you to get under their skin. No matter how much humour and seduction you use, they don't change and they are not swayed. It takes only a minute's worth of conversation before you realise you're not getting anywhere. This is illustrative of someone with firm boundaries, who stays in the shade and is perfectly content to be there. They didn't say anything, and it's probably what they didn't say that clearly defined their personal line. It may seem harsh and you may feel rebuffed, but at least you know how the land lies. You can sense their bubble and it's impermeable.

Here is a perfect illustration inspired by an old Buddhist tale that will help give you a bubble over the top of you to protect you from the sunrays. The Buddha was approached by a vile man who had heard that the Buddha will always love people, even if they were abusive. He didn't believe it but set out to prove it. He found the Buddha and let out a torrent of abuse, raging and spewing depravity. The Buddha listened and, when the man finally stopped, he said to him, 'If a man declined to accept the gift offered to him, who would it belong to?' The man replied, 'It would belong to the person who offered it, of course.' The Buddha said, 'My son, you have screamed at me, but I decline to accept your abuse and ask you to keep it for yourself. As the echo belongs to the sound, and the shadow to the substance, so misery will overtake the evildoer without fail.'

When you sit in the shade, you're out of the burning rays of the sun. All too often society rejects the notion of moving away from the high temperatures of life: 'If you can't stand the heat, get out the kitchen!' It implies that moving away from the heat is for wimps. But it's the opposite: staying in the heat is immature and for fighters. Fighting with others burns you up more quickly than anything else. It's a playground tactic, and it's an unnecessary diversion from getting that Beach Life. Moving into the shade is leaving your life's dramas behind and living with balance and stability. If you think about the upsets you've had, you find they usually include your attempts to change someone or their attempts to change you. Have you ever felt that disappointment when a lover hasn't turned out as you'd hoped? Or someone else telling you that they can't be/live with you the way you are? That's classic playground behaviour and joining in leads to a win/lose situation: someone's got to win and someone's got to lose.

But moving into the shade doesn't mean you're a doormat. Far from it. It means you're autonomous. Autonomy is self-governance: living your life according to your own rules. You step away from the herd mentality and no longer feel the need to conform to what others think you should do. If you are clear about your own boundaries and you have expressed them, verbally or through your behaviour, you have moved into the shade and out of the burning rays. And, in the safety of the shade, you become more confident because you trust your own intuition.

Ironically, you connect with people more readily because you know that they cannot hurt you. The very reason you went into the shade heals you so that, when you're ready, you can come back out into the sun as and when you desire. You enjoy others more because you have a safe place to recuperate when necessary. You can laugh more readily as you step out of the dramas and giggle from a distance. Those who meet the Dalai Lama often comment on how much he giggles. Many enlightened people giggle through life and these are the giggles of joy.

The Path of Least Resistance

'The goal of life is living in agreement with nature.'

Zeno of Citium (333–264 BCE), philosopher

When you're on holiday, you tend to take the path of least resistance. This describes the pathway that provides the least resistance to forward motion by an object or entity. A river, for example, will always take the path of least resistance as it is pulled downwards by gravity. Electricity behaves similarly. Taking the path of least resistance describes, in human terms, the path with least difficulty.

On holiday, taking the path of least resistance is liberating. You do what feels good and what feels right. You're less encumbered by expectations and you move smoothly through the day. You get up when you want and move through the day at your own pace. What's more fun: exploring the town or sitting by the pool? Whatever! You make the decision based on what gives you a warm feeling. There's no one to tell you what to do and, more importantly, you've stopped giving yourself that incessant monologue of what you *should* be doing. You're happy just being there, and the *doing* comes second.

Allowing your mind to become more settled is a gateway to stiller thoughts. Your conscious level will be carried down, away from the mind – a mental gravity, you could say. As you move towards those deeper levels, you become aware of another presence, which is often lost under the noise of mental chatter. It's much easier to become in tune with this part of yourself when you have the fewest expectations and least mind racing, and this is what feels so good about being on holiday.

Resistors

Of course, when you get home things change. You're back into the swing of 'normal' life. You have bills to pay, family to contend with and routines to keep to. It's easy to lose sight of that lovely mellow feeling back home. Or is it? Living on the path to least resistance back home is easier than you think. As soon as you get back you start putting up resistors that block the path of least resistance. These start as boulders and soon turn into a full-scale dam, which allows the water only to squeeze out. But, in removing these resistors, you will find your path flowing with less effort. In the table are some examples of resistors and their opposites.

Resistors	Path of least resistance
Other people's demands.	Taking responsibility for only what's yours.
Feeling overburdened.	Dropping unnecessary commitments.
Being stuck in a rut.	Stopping looking for things outside you to make you happy.
Having not enough money.	Decreasing your need to overspend.
Your marriage/relationship.	Becoming honest.
Fear.	Confronting it.
Your job.	Asking for challenges or finding another one.
Other people's criticisms.	Handing them back.

Perhaps you think removing these resistors is hard to do, but the point of the exercise is to understand that it's removing things from life that can lead to happiness, rather than looking elsewhere to find it. If you leave all the resistors in place, then expend more energy by trying to find another lover, make more money or get to the top of your career, you then have the resistors plus the added expectations of trying to change your outside life. Why not first consolidate your life as it is (by removing resistors), then consider what to add later?

As you feel the Stillness more and more, you will naturally move towards the path of least resistance. You will become more satisfied with less and you will learn to reduce your reliance on outside stimuli to increase happiness. This is the balance of nature.

It's easy to become stuck in your sense of what's 'normal' and what isn't. You have disallowed yourself choices because you are embedded in a culture that tells you what is expected of you. But this culture only an outpouring of someone else's thought process. This h culminated in the words of a thought process; the cover design that started as an idea; the chair on which v in someone's head; the house or flat you live in began as an idea; and the job you do was created by another person creating it in their mind. It's possible, through the Stillness, to see the outer world as simply the manifestation of other people's thoughts.

When you take the path of least resistance you are skipping a life of conscious conflict. Like the river winding its way around the boulders in the river, you can find the way through that feels most comfortable. The water that runs through the river will smooth the jagged edges of the boulders until they're even. Likewise, you can recreate this smoothness by allowing the very 'is-ness' of life to be. You will create an understanding of nonattachment, where you don't attach your identity to stuff outside of yourself. This is different from detachment, which is a pulling away. Think of a mother detaching the baby from its bottle versus a baby growing out of the need for its bottle – nonattachment.

Goals

'Shoot for the moon. Even if you miss, you'll land among the stars.'

Les Brown, life coach

There is a shift in modern consciousness from a goal-oriented world towards an evolution of waking up to another way to live – in the present. Stringent goal setting creates structures that keep people out of the present moment and chronically looking at the future. Whether these goals are destructive or helpful, long-term or short-term, is irrelevant. The exercise of looking towards the future before you can 'live' is a paradigm that works against the flow of life. It is the attachment of happiness to the goal that takes you away from living life as if it were one long holiday. That isn't to say you don't need goals, but it *is* saying that your attachment to the outcome is what propels you out of the moment.

When you're on holiday, you don't have the same attitude towards goals as you have back home. When you plan your day, you sketch out something you'd like to do: hire a bike, eat out, ramble into the hills. But, if your plans don't work out because something else comes along, it doesn't matter. You aren't attached to the outcome of your goals because they weren't written in stone. You have the 'holiday spirit' in you: *comme ci, comme ça*; *mañana*; maybe, maybe not!

Back home you may feel 'driven' by your goals. It's not the goals themselves that are the problem: it's that the goals are *driving* you that creates the stress. It's not possible to judge accurately your best interests for the future based on the restricted knowledge you have today. When you are directed by goals you have little room to manoeuvre. Because goals are fixed in their nature, you may restrict your natural creativity. You may wind up becoming rigid, inflexible or stuck. You can't come up with new ideas and discoveries outside your goal-controlled field of vision.

Goals also hinder the path of least resistance if they become compulsive. As with a drug, you can hang on to ineffective goals as a way of escaping your present situation. It's the old 'When I get there then everything will be OK' approach. It's a myth but being driven by goals can be completely justified by the established goal-driven society.

Have a look at this simple questionnaire to discover if you are goal-driven. Answer the questions 'yes' or 'no'. If you are unsure, leave them out.

Questions	Yes	No
Do you feel that you can't relax until you're in sight of achieving your goal?		
When you reach your goal, will you be happy?		
If you don't reach your goals, will you be very disappointed?		
Do you stay committed to your goals at any cost?		
Do you find yourself fixated on your goals?		
Are you waiting for the future to arrive before you can be happy?		

Do you feel something is missing from your life?		
Are you willing to stay frustrated now while you wait to achieve your goals in the future?		
Do others ask you if something is wrong when all you are doing is planning how to make your goals happen?		
Are you pushing ahead your goals to make someone else happy?		
Do you find it difficult to talk about things other than your goals?		

If you answer yes to three or more, you are goal-driven.

Just for a moment, imagine what your life would be like if you ditched all your goals. If the very idea of it has you feeling too uncomfortable, then it's illustrative of the point. Have you defined yourself through your goals? Your goals can become so deeply tied up with how you see yourself that you've forgotten the point of them and you no longer challenge them because the pressure to succeed among your peers is so strong. Think about it: are you following a path that evolved through some goals you set down years ago?

This could be liberation day, the day that you challenge your goals and ask yourself who or what you are doing it for! What are your morals, and are you working towards goals with those morals backing them up, or have your goals stayed the same while your morals have changed? Or are your goals limiting you by keeping you focused on the outcome with no space to breathe in the moment and feel the joy of simply being alive in the world today?

Intentions

The answer is not to *change* your goals but to have no *attachment* to your goals. Everyone has goals, even if it is 'to be happy'. However, if you hang on to that goal *no matter what*, you set up an obstacle on the path of least resistance. If you call your goal an intention, you are less attached to the outcome. Setting out intentions is a much easier way of living life. The path of least resistance will help you to interpret your intention in a way that flows more directly. Because you are not *attached* to a result but have a *preferred* outcome, you allow a lot more creativity to flow through your intentions. You won't be disappointed if your intention delivers something other than what you had in mind. You can afford to trust the outcome more than if you were fixed on a goal. This frees up creativity and energy that you can divert into allowing life to flow, because it's an assumption rather than a prediction.

Once you have laid down your intentions, you can let them go in order to come back into the present moment. Here is an example.

An intention: I would like my next job to increase my salary by a third.

Once you have put that intention in place, you are free to be as creative as possible while working towards that intention. If it were a goal, you would feel the pressure to deliver results in order to bag the job. It's simply a different approach.

By setting down your life's intentions, you will begin to live your whole life in the path of least resistance. You won't be focused on getting the river to flow down one channel only but you'll be allowing it to meander and create new streamlets. Your awareness will go beyond goals and they will have less pull on you. You will allow life to deliver to you rather than trying to pull out of it. Resisting and opposing will lessen and your tension will decrease. When your awareness is free to be more and more in the Stillness, you attract the powerful radiance from an inner source of life.

Through goals and planning, our minds prompt us to live in the future. Our present is focused on where we think we want to be and how to get there, rather than where we are. Never mind that the first thing we usually do when we reach our goal is rush out and get new goals, with barely a moment's time to reflect on our accomplishments.

The mind uses goals and plans in order to stay in charge. Our minds do this in order to protect us from the fear of uncertainty. But that protection comes in the form of lies. The mind lies when it tells us that it knows what life we will want in one month, six months or three years. The mind lies when it tells us that it knows the exact consequences of our actions. But they are seductive lies that give us an illusion of safety. In exchange for this illusion, we allow our minds to keep running the show.

As you begin setting intentions and letting go of goals, the mind will want to treat an intention like a goal. The mind will want to be specific, so that it knows exactly when the intention has manifested itself. It will want to make sure that the process of setting the intention has worked. It will expect results. But, when we're living through intention, there is no 'there' to get to. It is an ongoing dance of setting your intention and witnessing the response of the universe, so that you may then refine your intentions. This is how you hone your highest path and purpose. By letting go of knowing exactly what this path will look like when you get there, you find that it actually reveals itself perfectly, one moment at a time.

Create Your Intention

Take a moment. Bring your awareness into your body. Now think of your intention and visualise it perfectly. An intention is simply a thought, a wish or a desire. As you think of your intention, link it into the moment and feel what it feels like to have reached the intention. You are generating energy with your intention. The energy you create combines with the rest of the energy present in the universe. Fill the universe like ripples on a lake extending out to the edge until it flows over the entire lake.

The Shoreline

'We all make our limits, and we set them further out than we have any right.'

Robert Jordan, writer

Accepting the Limits

If you've ever stayed in a small beach resort, you'll know there is limited potential for what you can get up to. That said, it's not a bad thing. In fact, it can be the making of your holiday. You've come to relax and your options are: beach, bar, Zorro and his boat, three restaurants, a visit to the local vineyard and one church to explore. So, what do you do?

Well, if you had been expecting a resort with four-star restaurants, the whole beach caboodle with jet skis and water skiing and all-singing, all-dancing evening entertainment, then you might have been a little disappointed. But, as it is, you can't change it so you just get down to enjoying what you've got.

You make the most of it by easing into the life of getting up – whenever – and moseying down to the beach for a swim. Perhaps some tapas at the beach bar before heading back to the hotel for a shower and a lie-down. Later you explore one of the three restaurants for some nifty local grub and a few beers, mingling with the small crowds where the locals outnumber the tourists by fifty to one.

By the end of your holiday you find that not only did you accept that the holiday wasn't going to be as you'd hoped, but it actually turned out to be a whole lot *better* than you planned. What a bonus!

Embracing your Limits

We live in a society that positively endorses self-improvement. You are to 'realise' your dreams at any cost and eliminate any negative feelings that stand in your way. The prolific talent shows that are springing up act like a pulse on this 'anyone can be a star' thinking. When a contestant is told that they don't have any talent they are incredulous, sometimes to the point of becoming abusive.

There is a billion-dollar industry marketed to people who are trying to make their impossible dreams come true with titles that mould around themes such as: live your dreams; make it happen; dream and grow rich; and so on. Clairvoyants 'predict' futures while hypnotists 'refocus' you to go and crack the industry so you can get the top job. Books tell you to ask the universe to make all your dreams come true while websites reel off ways to manifest riches. While there is some nobility in helping others' dreams come true, more often that not it is unrealistic to push people into trying to achieve things that they will never achieve.

'Never give up!' is the message that's being thrown around, and this means never admit failure. But the reality is that many dreams never come true and hanging on to the impossible is going to make you *feel* like a failure. This can seem like such a slap in the face for many in a culture that thoroughly endorses fighting to change the reality of our lives. Self-reliance, 'courage beyond words' and stepping outside your comfort zone might seem like lion-heart sentiments, but, in spite of everything, if your dream doesn't come true, you may come to feel ashamed and guilty.

Let's say you have dreams of getting your screenplay made into a film. You send it out to several film companies – not a word back! You send out some more and try to find an agent. Not only do you hear nothing back from the film companies but no agent will take you on as a client until you've got at least one screenplay accepted as an option by a film house. You're determined because your friends and family have said, in fact *everyone* has said, how brilliant the script is. You take the script and knock on the doors of the production companies but no one will even look at it. You're wound up, frustrated and heavily disappointed. You carry on for a few more months, but, after sending out the 42nd package with no response, you begin to accept that perhaps your script wasn't ever going to become the next Oscar winner.

The hardest thing to do is accept your limits. To say 'I can't and never will' is true courage. It may feel hard to accept at first but, once you have embraced your limits, things change. Accepting that you may never realise your childhood dreams involves grief and indulging in the grief is a good way to wash away the harsh realities of life. And the payoff is great, too. Here's what will happen as a result.

- You stop feeling like a victim.
- You no longer feel that life's unfair.
- Your dejection will lift.
- You feel better in yourself.
- You feel free to get on with other things.
- You find a new creativity you didn't know you had.
- New opportunities pop up that you'd not seen before.
- You write another script for fun, not to sell.
- You feel lighter.
- You're happier because you're not waiting to sell the script to be happy.
- You have more time because you're not obsessing about your dreams.

There may be many areas of your life in which you are waiting for things to happen before you can be happy. It's worth investigating, because your unfulfilled dreams could be making you despondent. Take a little time to note down all those dreams you've been hanging on to that you know, in your heart, are probably not going to come true. These could be hoping that a certain person will fall in love with you, that you become a film star, that you buy the house of your dreams or win the lottery.

Once you have identified your dreams, be realistic about which ones will come true. Tick off the ones that probably won't come true and say goodbye to them. Hankering after these dreams when there's little hope of realising them can hold you back from really getting the life you want. Because you are constantly living in the future, you don't allow the joy of the present moment to flourish.

Embracing limits is a profound and uplifting experience. The pressure to perform, manipulate and control has gone. Another door has opened and it has no conditions attached to it. By saying 'this is as good as it gets', you are accepting your limits with self-assurance and respect.

Radical Acceptance

Not accepting your limits keeps you in a state of chronic anxiety because you focus on trying to achieve what you probably will never achieve. The antidote to this is radical acceptance. Radical acceptance is a way to cut through the all the confusion that comes from trying to achieve the impossible. In fact, it cuts into the core like a hot knife through butter. It gives you the choice between staying locked into an indeterminate future and being free of its control. When you go on holiday, you are likely to leave behind the chaos and suffering that go with living in a future dream. It teaches you to do this every day of your life.

Radical acceptance focuses on what you know to be true rather than what you are not certain of and what you can't control. What you know is what is true in the present moment. If you accept the truth – now – you can embrace it with all of your senses, heart, intellect, feelings, thoughts and so on. By simply noticing, without judging, your moment-by-moment awareness, you become an observer of the hub of yourself. As you stay with each moment and notice the sensations in your body, you will find that the sensations lessen and radical acceptance will filter through. You are not judging the sensation to be good: you are accepting the sensation in spite of your desires.

If you find the sensations to be gruelling, soothe yourself through your five senses. Here's some examples.

- **Touch:** Take a luxurious bath, put on your favourite sweater, snuggle up to a pet, get a massage, hug someone or prepare your bedroom for sleep.
- **Taste:** Eat a delicious meal, eat your favourite sweet and savour every moment, eat something you know you shouldn't and enjoy every mouthful.

- **Smell:** Buy yourself a gorgeous flower and put it by your bed, put some lavender oil on your pillow, light a scented candle.
- **Sound:** Listen to natural sounds such as a waterfall or birds singing, or put on some soothing music.
- **Vision:** Go for a walk in a lovely park or forest, watch the flames in a fire and take in the stars and the moon.

When you think about being on holiday, you tend to use more of your senses than when you're at home. This could be a brilliant contributor to that sensual holiday feeling because you're so in tune with yourself and nature. By soothing yourself through your senses you are regaining some of those sumptuous feelings that you get when you're on holiday.

Another method of soothing yourself is to make a note of the reasons why you are practising radical acceptance. For example, write down the positive consequences of radical acceptance, such as feeling in control, lifting depression and relieving pressure, and imagine how good you are going to feel once those reasons have gone. Now write down the negative consequences of not practising radical acceptance, such as what you do to run from your emotions (drinking, spending money, drugs or other compulsive behaviour). Keep these two poles in mind but focus on the first one and how great you will feel when this temporary anguish passes.

To live life with radical acceptance seems tricky at first. You may feel as though you keep stumbling on a path full of boulders that trip you up. But always remember, the feelings *will* pass and you will be amazed how great you feel afterwards. It's much harder always being 'on the run' into the future and escaping from your emotions, and that leads to exhaustion, stress and/or depression. Practising radical acceptance is a much easier way to live life and will bring you faster into the Beach Life type of living that you were hoping to find when you picked up this book. It gets easier the more you practise. And, wow, is it worth it!

REPACKING YOUR BAG: REFLECTION

Have you had that experience of packing your bag on the day you leave your holiday destination and you've got all those good feelings rushing around you and you're calm, serene and contented? A lot of that 'Zen-ness' is easily replicated back home. The following passages take the essence of the holiday boosts and discuss the ways to implement the same ideas back home. They require no effort and they're not demanding. It simply boils down to seeing it another way.

Travelling En-lightened

'To be enlightened is to be free.'

Anonymous

Travelling light is an art form. The best way to travel is without any bags at all, and, if you're one of those who can get away with just a carry-on, you're blessed. For the rest of us, well, there's excess baggage! Remember when you packed to go on holiday? You sat on the bag and, against the odds, you had to get everything in plus the emergency extras. Inch by inch, you forced the zip around until it reached the end and then you snapped the buckles down before it changed its mind.

Once you were en route you realised how fortunate you were to have only the one bag because two would have definitely weighed you down. Once you got to your destination and unpacked the case, you realised how satisfying it was to have just what you needed. Lo and behold, halfway through your holiday you exclaimed to yourself, 'I didn't need *half* of this stuff!' and resolved to cut your excess baggage next holiday.

Learning to live with what you need with no extra fat on the bone is a joy. Learning to live lighter feels lighter, right where it counts, inside. Think about how you felt on holiday and compare it with how you feel about your life back home. Do you feel as though your life at home is burdened with 'stuff' that you have to haul around, compared with that exquisite illuminated feeling that travelling on holiday gives you? Here are some tips to bring the holiday freshness back home.

Simplify Your Home

Do you think of your house as the setup for a great tabletop sale? You may have so much stuff lying around that you simply don't use and it's getting to feel cluttered. Think back to that villa or hotel room where you spent a good week with nothing more than the bare essentials. Which feels clearer? Living in a light house will help you feel lighter inside.

If your house is cluttered or messy, this will reflect in all areas of your life, and especially in your mind. Cluttered surroundings can make you feel messy and this leads to feeling overwhelmed. So get started by clearing and simplifying your home. Go through each room and take a look at the stuff that isn't necessary to make your life run smoothly. Ask yourself, 'Do I love it? Do I need it?' If not, get rid of it. A car-boot sale is such a great way to unburden your life and get paid for doing it. With the money, treat yourself to one new gorgeous thing for your home.

The more stuff you hang on to, the more space you need. The more space you need, the bigger the costs: extra insurance, storage, security and so forth. You don't need that extra weight to pull you down. Give it up; chuck it out! Feel yourself immediately breathing the clear space.

Lighten the Load

Once you get back from your holiday you're straight into your responsibilities: work, family, meetings, fitting in the gym, spending time with friends, hobbies, domestic chores, the extracurricular activities you've taken on in good faith, plus the fact that you're travelling to and from work at least an hour each way. Then there are the emails to be answered, shopping to be done, calls to be returned, texts to write and paperwork to attend to. And you mustn't forget to deal with all other problems, arrange your calendar, get balance in your life, accomplish all daily tasks and get to bed early. Phew!

Life has become too hectic. Have you ever fantasised about ditching your obligations and running back to the beach in Greece to take over the local bar? It sounds like liberation, doesn't it? But you really don't have to go to those lengths to create a lighter existence. And the chances are that you would only take your tendency to overburden yourself with you, and, before you know it, you're living the life of an overburdened manger of a Greek beach bar.

Here are two easy ways to lighten your load immediately: ditch the unnecessary and ask for help.

- **Ditch the unnecessary:** In the same way as you have lightened your house, ditch what you don't need or love. Are you taking on too many responsibilities for other adults? Drop commitments that don't nourish you and that you don't need to do.
- **Ask for help:** You may be amazed how you resist asking for help because you think the answer will be no or you think that no one else will do the job as well as you, so you end up carrying everything on your shoulders. But trying to do everything yourself is the fastest route to nowhere. If you think your responsibilities are eating into your time, ask for help, and you may find that others were glad to

be asked. Your competence may have given the impression you never needed any help!

Healing the Disease to Please

How many times in the last year have you said yes when you meant no? Saying yes when you mean no is a disease to please! This is a common trait yet a source of much angst and unnecessary burden. Constantly saying yes when you don't mean it can become a source of severe stress. When you're on holiday you are away from that familiar setting and you might feel the difference in the way you deal with people. Why is it when you get back home that you can't say no? Here are a few possible reasons why.

- You want to avoid an argument so you give in.
- You worry that the other person won't like you if you don't agree to what is being asked of you.
- You're concerned that someone else will be hurt by your declining.
- You think you'll be left out if you don't say yes.
- You want to feel virtuous by doing what is asked of you.

Is it possible that you are taking on the role of a doormat and allowing others to take advantage of you? Here are some of the downsides of the disease to please.

- You secretly feel resentful.
- Stress is getting the better of you.
- You have to lie continually to keep up the pretence that you're keen to do what you've agreed to.
- You blow up at those around you because you're drained and angry.
- You complain to others about the people you say yes to.

Here are some ways to deal with others that may help you to heal your need to please.

Practise saying no. This many not come easily at first, so start with a small no and work up.

Buy yourself some time with stock phrases such as 'I'll take that away and think about it' or 'Thanks for asking – I'll get back to you on that.' Simple phrases that you have to hand can get you out of needing to respond straightaway.

If you're afraid that someone will become angry if you say no, remember that you have every right to say no, as they have every right to ask. As you practise, your confidence will increase and you won't allow yourself to be manipulated. Continual self-sacrifice is demeaning; growing self-respect is exciting.

Remember, you are not powerful enough to make someone like you. Start being true to yourself and you will come across as authentic, and that's such a charismatic and personable trait.

Saying yes when you mean no is a way of ultimately appeasing yourself. Are you avoiding others' attention or looking for an easy life by saying yes? By dropping the need to please, you are becoming more honest with yourself and others, and that can only lead to a more fulfilling life.

Update Your Address Book

Do you spend time with people whose negative attitude you could do without? You know the ones: people who are always right, tell you you're doing it wrong or simply talk about themselves all the time. You hang out with them out of habit but you don't look forward to seeing them. A holiday can give you the chance to reassess your relationships as well as providing a much-needed break from those people you could do without. Take an honest look at these people. Which friends do you enjoy and which friends drag you down?

Good friends are worth their weight in gold. It's worth putting in the time and energy to nurture those relationships. But this takes time, and everyone's limited in how much time they have going. This is a good time to bow out gracefully from those relationships that do you no favours.

But there are some relationships you have to continue, even though you don't like them. This is a good occasion to look at what obstacles are in the way of your getting on with those you need to maintain good relationships with: family, colleagues, in-laws, parents of your children's friends, your children themselves. These relationships can be a minefield of emotional turmoil but keeping an eye on that holiday feeling will help you to be a little more objective about what you can do to change things.

Doing your part to maintain healthy relationships requires you to speak the truth. This doesn't mean a full-on appraisal of them every time you meet, but, if you start with 'I' instead of 'you', you are halfway there. For example, rather than telling another person how they should run their life, you could tell them how you feel about your own. Opening up and telling someone else about your ups and downs is a cleaner way to communicate. It also softens you and gives the other person a chance to talk more honestly about themselves.

And let's take a look at the word *integrity*. It sums up the truth as you know it. And it means that you tell the truth as you know it. It means you are the same inside as you are outside. It means you present yourself in an honest way. As you move towards the Stillness, becoming more integral will become easier. As you become more familiar with the warm place inside you, you will become more self-assured. You will not feel the need to 'sell' yourself as much but your natural inclination will lean towards having fun. You will become more enjoyable to be around because you will get pleasure from just being with people. Your relationships will feel lighter and you will laugh more, just as you do when you're on holiday.

The Competition Commission

'My grandfather once told me that there were two kinds of people: those who do the work and those who take the credit. He told me to try to be in the first group; there was much less competition.'

Indira Gandhi (1917–1984), Indian politician

Have you noticed how you feel much warmer towards other people when you are on holiday? You share a smile, rather than a grunt; you feel more tolerant and more easygoing; you enjoy others' company in a way that you just don't at home. This is especially true of people who are local to your holiday destination. They seem flamboyant and unusual and you love watching and admiring them. Sitting in a local café watching the world and its people go by is an enchanting, ideal way to spend a morning. Even your holiday neighbours are fascinating and you pay attention to them, curious and intrigued.

The reason for this? You have stepped out of the Competition Commission, the 'race of your life', and you are running a fair competition. Being competitive with others is one sure way to keep from feeling great. As long as you are comparing yourself to others, it's a competition you are never going to win and a sure-fire way of keeping the good feelings away.

So how and why does this competition take place? We live in a world where the best 'win', or do they? Living your life to be better than the next is exhausting and unrewarding. While you stand on the podium at the end of the race, waving your trophy in the air, the crowds will be dispersing back to a life that doesn't require a victory to give them a good day. In fact, it was the watching and clapping that was the fun bit. Noncompetitive people don't need to make themselves seem bigger, taller, more intelligent, better-looking, wealthier or more entertaining than anyone else – they leave that to others, because it simply adds a stress that they could better do without.

As long as you are in the race, you will find that, no matter how many races you win, as soon as you have walked away from the winners' podium you will have your eye on the next race. This feeling of competition does not become sated with wins, and you will never win enough competitions to satisfy yourself. The competition is a state of mind, not a goal to achieve. We need competitions in our world to help perpetuate change. But, if your part in the race is causing you to feel your life is worthless because you are not winning, then it may be time to take another look at the value of the competition. Is the prize money high enough for you to take part?

Consider this: when you are competing, you are competing to win; if you win then someone has to lose, and your good feelings will be the opposite of someone's bad feelings! We tend to stare with open mouths at the colossal amounts of money the City populace makes. Those bonuses of millions might have you slavering, dreaming of the lifestyle you could enjoy. The people who earn these fortunes work like dogs and will log on to their Blackberries all night long to ensure the deal. Ask them if they are happy. Ask them if they are fulfilled. Do they have a Beach Life? Possibly not, but, if you are one of them, do not despair.

You Have to be a Somebody Before You Can Become a Nobody

There is an old Buddhist saying: 'You have to be somebody before you can become nobody.' You have to know yourself before you can blend into the world. This may mean letting your ego run wild, racing with other egos and establishing just where it will come in the race. You may discover you're a thirteen-out-of-fifty type or an unfailing first-every-time type. No matter, what you achieve helps you to adjust by getting to understand your limits and your boundaries. You may need to feel sated with being a somebody before you can relax into being a nobody.

Being a nobody is the Zen of living. Once you've established who you are and what you can achieve, you become ready to let go of your ego. This doesn't mean you need to pack up your life and move to the mountains and live in a cave with the siddhas. This means that you are ready to let go of the attachment to outer success as the path to happiness, compulsive thinking or clinging to an identity in order to shore up your ego. It means you don't have to give up anything except the compulsive thinking and the attachment to success.

As you move into the Stillness you will feed your ego state through another door. You will feed yourself with the food of life: bliss, creativity and harmony. The angst and constant tension of holding up the structure, which houses the false ego, melts into the river of alertness. And all the energy that was being used to maintain this structure is released into the art of being alive. You don't need to make a conscious effort to do this by giving up everything you are trying to achieve. If you simply bring yourself into the moment as and when you remember, you will be nourished each time you access it.

You will recognise that this is the feeling you get when you are on holiday. It's the feeling that you have stepped away from the race that has been driving you around in circles, and the 'What a relief not to have to be in it!' feeling just for the moment. The nourishment you receive from the Stillness will be enough to help you to let go of the need to win at all costs.

Keeping Body and Soul Together

'The body is the shell of the soul, and dress the husk of that shell; but the husk often tells what the kernel is.'

Robert Southey (1774–1843), poet

The connection between body and soul goes way beyond eating your allotted fruit and vegetables every day and pacing yourself through a gruelling workout in the gym three times a week. The body-and-soul connection goes to a level deeper than your conscious awareness. You know that razzing it up at a really good party one night leaves you with the mother of all hangovers the next day. Or a week of a tried-and-trusted health kick when nothing unhealthy passes your lips makes you feel fabulous as well as sanctimonious. But this is different.

The Food Effect

Eating cleaner food equates to a cleaner body. A cleaner body equates to feeling better. Feeling better equates to more happiness. But it's not just *what* you eat that counts, but the way you eat and drink that has a profound effect on body and soul.

Life's a beach

First, it's important to be mindful of the connection between body and soul when eating. Being mindful means to sense the fullness of your attention to the food with an undisrupted presence. Imagine yourself eating a pear by grabbing it as you run out of the door and chomping it down in the car before you get to the next junction, when you're going to need both hands on the wheel. Then imagine eating it slowly while paying attention to its taste, smell and the feel of it in your hand as you savour each mouthful, all the while appreciating its deliciousness.

Being mindful of your food will help to bring you more into the Stillness. Fully focusing your mind while eating helps to soothe you and bring your focal point into your body. As you eat, your concentration is purposeful, focusing on what is going on inside. Being aware of your food, even if it is junk food, is being mindful. It's a way of connecting your mind and body in the present moment.

Apart from the quality of the food you're eating, it's important to be mindful of where the food has come from. You could be eating in a glamorous restaurant with a string of stars after its name, but if the person who is paying is trying to 'buy' your favour then the food could taste 'contaminated'. In this instance you may connect the food to an uncomfortable situation and this will disturb your senses. However, if you have cooked the simplest meal at home and your purpose was to nourish your body, then eating that meal settles your senses.

It's wonderful to be on holiday and to explore the food market for local delicacies, taking them back to your apartment/tent/villa and cooking them with only a few other ingredients because that's all you have. Or deliberating over which restaurant you want to eat in – and, oh, the choice is amazing! A meal eaten under these circumstances brings a new mindfulness in the way you eat. It's almost certainly not in front of the TV, but is probably eaten in good company, eaten gently and eaten all in good time.

As you move more and more into the Stillness, you will become much more attuned to the connection between how you eat and the way you feel. Of course, it's not always possible to eat mindfully, but this book isn't telling you to change the way you eat. It's the other way round. When you tune into the present you will become more mindful about what and how you eat.

You can become so in tune with your body that you feel the effect of certain foods in specific areas of your body. For example, when you have two or three glasses of wine, or more alcohol than you are used to, you will notice your heart racing more than usual; if you have eaten very rich food you may have a sensation under your right ribs where your liver is doing its best to break the food down. Conversely, you may have eaten a light, clean mean with grains and pulses and you can feel the food working through your digestive system, cleaning it like a gentle brush as it works its way down.

The more in tune with your body you become, the more of a friend it becomes to you. You can calm your soul by calming your body. And, before you throw your hands in the air, saying, 'What a load of hippie claptrap!' consider this. You are doing it anyway. Every time you eat a white-bread, cheese-and-pickle sandwich with a bag of crisps and a coffee, think about how you feel. Are you jumping with energy or are you feeling lethargic and a little low? You have the body-and-soul connection happening anyway so, you may as well turn it to your advantage.

The Rhythm of the Universe

Everything works to a rhythm. The universe hums with a cadence as the stars pulse and the planets rotate. This rhythm reverberates through all of life: the sun's rising and setting, the moon's orbit around the Earth, Earth's orbit around the sun, the cycle of the seasons, sleep and activity, the beat of the heart, the fertility cycle, the rest-and-activity rhythm, rocking a baby, breathing, life and death. We are programmed to respond to the rhythm of the universe. Our whole life moves with rhythm. When we get up in the morning we have begun the rhythmic process. We sleep and wake, work and rest, eat and excrete, laugh and cry.

As you move further into the body, you become more in tune with the rhythm inside. You will sense when you need rest and recuperation because you feel the vibration inside you sounding a little on the high side. You will also sense when your body is calling for more exercise because your natural flow is inhibited through a lack of flexibility or a feeling of extra weight on your heart. If you feel heavy in your stomach you could be in tune with your digestive system as it calls for a clean (i.e. with less fat and salt) meal to brush out your tract.

Do you notice when your body is out of tune with the natural rhythm of life? This happens when you disregard your body's queries. If you exercise compulsively you may not be aware of the healing time it needs while muscles repair themselves. You may not be in tune with the body's need to be still if you are working excessively. Being on holiday can hone your senses, which will retune you to your body's rhythms. You can then bring that experience back home and take some time, every day, to feel the pulse of your body, which will help keep together your body and soul. Ask your body questions about what it requires to keep it on track. You'll be surprised by the answers.

Bringing Together Body and Soul

Merging the body and the soul is what happens on holiday. The very fact that you've got your clothes off and your swimsuit on means you are more in tune with your body. You're examining bits you hadn't seen since last year, slathering cream all over it, exercising it.

But are you aware of being attuned to it – in other words, feeling your body and soul at the same time? Here's a meditation to get you started on bringing them together.

Feeling the presence of your body

As you read the words on this page, instead of seeing them in the top of your head, see if you can focus the words down to the middle of your body. Make the source of the words emanate from your stomach. Close your eyes now if it makes it feel easier.

Focus all your attention on the centre of your body. Keep your attention focused right in the middle and imagine a small ball of light – about the size of a table-tennis ball.

Keep your attention on the light and make it grow to the size of a tennis ball. Now it's growing to the size of small melon. The light that comes out of it is fluid and radiant. Keep your focus on the source of the light but feel the light moving into your chest, neck, upper arms and down into your pelvis and now your thighs. Now feel it move into your hands, feet and head. Hold that sensation for a few minutes.

Can you feel the vibration of your body? Can you feel the energy from the light permeate every cell? Can you *feel* the experience instead of imagining it?

The energy that reverberates within your body is a phenomenon in itself. You can move that energy right around your body until your whole being feels light and uplifted. This energy will help to heal you as you begin the task of building a foundation of self-confidence and self-trust. It is the journey towards the very centre of you.

Until you feel the presence of your body, you are living a constant 'out-of-body' experience. If you have lived outside the body for most of your life, then you may struggle to feel your body's energy. In this case, ask the body what it needs to help your soul to re-inhabit it. Your body will tell you. Listen well.

If you find you cannot enter the body spontaneously because you are feeling an uncomfortable emotion when you concentrate on the body, do not fret. Check out the discomfort by letting your attention linger on to it. Let the light of your attention shine on it. Accept the pain and this will help to dislodge or dissolve it. If tears flow, let them come.

Being present in your body builds an anchor for your soul. If you do nothing else in this book, learning to live in your body instead of out of it can lead you to personal realisation. Don't underestimate its power. It's an exercise that you can build up over time. When you find yourself with a couple of minutes to spare, sitting in a traffic jam or on the Tube, bring your attention into your body until you feel its vibration again. You will find yourself spontaneously doing this after a relatively short period of time. And it's quite amazing how much you feel physically better after bringing your attention into the body.

Money, Money, Money

'A bank is a place that will lend you money if you can prove that you don't need it.'

Bob Hope (1903–2003), comedian

Money, money, money – you love it, hate it, bend over backwards to make it. It makes you happy, lack of it makes you miserable, you can live without it but you hate to need it. Regardless of how we feel about it, money rules our lives.

When you go on holiday you have a different relationship with money. First, you find the best exchange rate to change your hard-earned cash for a local wedge. You've worked out what you'll need beforehand, so you're well covered for the week. Once you've got your wedge, you spend fairly wisely because you've got a certain amount to last you the whole holiday and you really don't want to get your credit card out if you can help it. While you're spending your money you're thinking hard about how much everything costs because (1) you've got a set amount to spend and (2) you're continually mentally changing the cash back into your own currency in your head to work out how much you would be spending back home.

Emotional Money

The relationship we have with money is tricky. We want it but we don't want to be seen to want it. Yet the advertisers promise to trade us happiness for our hard-earned cash. But, in not having enough, we can feel debilitated, less than everyone else or unworthy as a person. In some circles it's seen as a sin to yearn for more money but in others money is a god.

We are constantly bombarded by media messages about how we should live our lives according to the amount of money we spend. If we look at property, move into a new house with a kitchen that's five or more years old, there's a general assumption that we'll be replacing the kitchen as soon as possible. A car without electric windows or air conditioning is now seen as 'odd'. Teenagers think nothing of spending several hundred pounds on the handbag or trainers of the moment and in some teen circles that's cheap! Money has become easy to borrow and even easier to spend and it has fostered an uneasiness in us.

Money has been translated into a fantasy of happiness. For some people, money can become the crux of compulsive behaviour because it stimulates a craving for personal security and, like a fantasy, it never has an ending. Money becomes a 'problem' when people spend to change the way they feel, get the spending 'high', suffer the comedown and need to spend more to feel good. It's a cycle, which ends in unhappiness because it never works; spending to feel good leaves the spender feeling worse – and in debt!

Once in debt, you are so far from the good feelings that go with that delicious holiday feeling that you may need to spend more to run away from the guilt and anxiety. That anxiety leads to stress, which has a similar effect to foods that act as a stimulant, such as chocolate, coffee, highly sweetened foods and fizzy drinks. The 'buzziness' is a response to the overstimulation of the nervous system and this acts as a physical barrier to feeling calm and becoming still, which is where the inner peace is found. As luck would have it, the very act of overspending to feel better actually sets us back in our search for happiness and creates a cycle of unhappiness.

The More-and-more Effect

There's also a growing concern that there's never going to be enough, which makes us search out more ways to make more money. Everyone's looking for a bigger piece of the pie. It's as if there were a famine coming, but the irony is that the *seeking* takes us into 'when I get there I'll be happy' territory, and that leads to unhappiness. There is a myth that more money creates more fulfilment, but this is as hollow as a cheap chocolate egg and there is no evidence for it.

The craving for more money creates chronic unhappiness because the craving will never be fulfilled no matter how much money is available. Money is one commodity that creates more and more longing, the more it's spent. What is the craving really stemming from? A desire to be accepted (by buying more peer-savvy stuff)? A need to be admired (by doing stuff that others admire)? A craving to be loved (by buying grown-up 'sweets' and 'toys')? A need to feel worthy (by gaining respect from others)?

Take this quiz to check out your spending habits.

Question	Always	Sometimes	Never
I don't know how much I spent last month until my credit-card bill arrives.			
I buy things spontaneously.			
I spend at least 20 per cent of my take-home pay on credit cards.			
I always spend the money in my account.			
I hide some purchases from at least one other person.			

I want something but I don't know if I have the money to buy it.			
I don't have an accurate record of what I've bought.			
I always want more than I have.			
I never seem to have enough money even though I earn a good amount.			
I'm unsure how much my monthly expenses are.			
If I earn more I automatically upgrade my lifestyle.			
I don't know exactly what my outstanding credit-card debts are.			
I don't take advantage of all offers.			
I never have a surplus amount of money at the end of the month.			
I save less than 10 per cent of my net income.			
I buy things I never use.			

Add up how many instances of 'always', 'sometimes' and 'never' you ticked and decide which one outweighs the others. How did you score?

Mostly never – mindful spender
Congratulations! You are a mindful spender. You balance living within your means with still having fun with your money. You can sleep well at night knowing that your happiness is not spend-dependant.

Mostly sometimes – fun spending
You're halfway there! You're somewhere between trying to keep up with your peers and wanting to be debt-free. Be more aware of where

your money is going and set yourself spending plans and stick to them. Don't be fooled into thinking that spending more will make you happier.

Mostly always – emotional spender

Listen up! Stumbling through your financial life means you won't get the Beach Life you're looking for. You may be heading for trouble, so do yourself a favour and get your financial life in order now. You may be someone who mistakes spending for feeling good, but ignoring your debts is not going to help. You don't want to be working long after everyone else has gone home.

Here are some top tips to curb your spending:

Admit to your overspending: It takes great courage to admit you overspend. Look behind your spending and establish the hole you're trying to fill. Is it loneliness, feeling 'less than' others, running from sadness or something else? There is a reason for overspending; it's not isolated. Don't let money become a no-go subject.

Occupy yourself at home: Start a new hobby at home. It's amazing how getting busy at making things takes your mind off spending money. You may even *earn* some money.

Give yourself a 'go-mad' budget: Set out a sum of money each month to go mad with. This varies with each person but when it's gone it's gone!

Consider how much work it took you to afford what you're going to buy: This is a great way to weigh up and value what you're buying. If it took you half a day to earn those twenty cappuccinos from Starbucks you might think twice about buying them.

A great way to fritter money: Take five pounds to the pound shop.

Wait for several days before you buy something: Your memory is short. You may have forgotten about it if you sleep on it. The shopping lust soon wanes.

Every time you stop yourself from buying something you

don't need, save it: Watching the sums grow in your saving account is a buzz in itself.

Don't buy stuff just because it's a bargain: It's a bargain only if you were going to buy it anyway.

Spend cash only: Because you always spend more on a card.

Unclutter and you'll find you have what you need. Check out what you already own. When you realise how much stuff you already have, it may quell your desire to go out spending. If you buy new things you have to put them somewhere; you may need to display them so then you have to buy furniture or shelves to put them on show or drawers and cabinets in which to leave them. Next time you feel like a spending spree, unclutter a room instead. It will give you more satisfaction and you may find some old treasures you had forgotten about.

But Money's Not a Dirty Word

Think of it like this: long ago, before there was money, people survived by building their own houses, searching for water, hunting for food and making clothes from animal skins. Life was about pure survival. If you wanted anything over and above what you produced, you would trade something you had for something that someone else had.

The drawback is that you had to be in the same place at the same time to exchange goods. Since this was impractical, money was invented to get round this problem and match the value of your goods or services with someone else's goods and services. It was an amazing invention and it meant you didn't have to be always in the same place to swap goods.

With that idea in mind, it's time to reassess your views on money and how they balance up with the soul. Many spiritual leaders don't talk about money in a spiritual way. But here's the thing: if you had the chance of flying to Australia, would you choose economy seats or first-class seats? Yep, the first-class seats are going to win. Or, if you decide to eat out, would you want to go to the local pub and have a sandwich, or would you like to sample some beautiful food that is prepared to a high standard in a restaurant? Of course, dining out and eating some delicious fresh food is far preferable. It's an exquisite pleasure and one that having more money can make possible. It's a way in which money can be spent soulfully.

The best exchange rate happens when you don't exchange your peace of mind for the high-end pressure of making loads of money. It's a matter of finding the exchange rate that gives you enough without making you compromise your tranquillity.

It's only human to want more comfort rather than less, and that's where having enough money is comfortable. When you go on holiday, you want to eat nice food, buy a holiday souvenir and be able to get the taxi to the local historical monument; after that, everything else is a bonus. After all, just being on holiday is good enough. And that's the key – good enough.

Your Money or Your Life?

So, pondering the balance of the scales, *having enough* is the way to go. If you live and earn enough to give you enough, you're on to a winner. You have the stability of not needing to kill yourself to keep body and soul together, so you can kick back and spend more time pondering the Stillness, which nourishes you and gives you the Beach Life feeling. That's not to say you need to have your scales balanced before you can touch the Stillness, but it does mean that you don't need to spend any more time than is necessary in the future.

For many people, it's not that they don't have enough: it's that they don't *realise* they have enough to get that Beach Life feeling. Many people live life thinking they need more and more to enjoy blissful living, but this is an illusion. Working towards having enough is the way to living a happier life.

The Best Exchange Rate

To get a handle on your craving to spend, simply exchange your craving for the Stillness. It's life's best possible exchange rate. As soon as you turn your attention into the Stillness, you will feel satisfied. That's all it takes. Tuning into the present moment takes away all the craving and desire you have to fill yourself up with *things*.

Having enough is having as much as you need to live comfortably. It means knowing your limits and respecting them. Having enough means not having to justify your actions to anyone else. It means you're at peace with what you have and how you spend your wealth. Having enough is being satisfied with what you've got and knowing what you need to surround yourself with to make you snug. It may mean giving some away if you've got more than you need.

But you don't want just to be comfortable: you also want to thrive. Here is a diagram, devised by Abraham Maslow (1908–70), an eminent psychologist, which explains our lists of needs to thrive to the best of our potential. It is known as Maslow's Hierarchy of Needs.

At the bottom of the pyramid are our physiological needs – rock-bottom survival needs for air, water, food, shelter and sleep. The second layer contains safety and security needs – our need for a sense of security in a predictable world with a relative absence of threat to

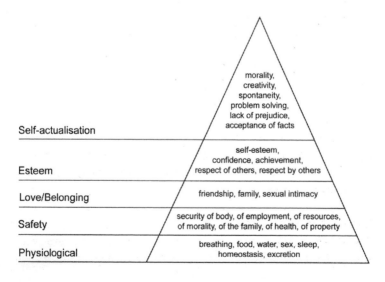

Self-actualisation	morality, creativity, spontaneity, problem solving, lack of prejudice, acceptance of facts
Esteem	self-esteem, confidence, achievement, respect of others, respect by others
Love/Belonging	friendship, family, sexual intimacy
Safety	security of body, of employment, of resources, of morality, of the family, of health, of property
Physiological	breathing, food, water, sex, sleep, homeostasis, excretion

ourselves. The third layer designates love and belongingness needs – our need for warm, interpersonal sharing, love and affection, and affiliation. The fourth layer designates self-esteem and esteem by others – our need for a sense of confidence and competence, achievement, independence and freedom. At the top of the pyramid are self-actualisation needs – our need for growth, development, utilisation of potential, i.e. to become more and more what we are capable of becoming.

Once you have your comfort needs in place, then you can aspire to fulfilling your relationships and work-potential desires. Once these steps are in place, it is a lot easier to bring in money from a job that offers more significance than simply earning a wage. You don't continually have to ask yourself, 'Is it my money or my life?'

If you have more than enough, then you have a bonus – the cherry on the cake. You will recognise that having more than enough is a privilege to do with what you like. Once you have established that you have the income to support your life in which you have 'enough', you could think about working less and be happier doing other things. You may enjoy working less – less 'doing', more 'being'. The possibilities are captivating. Consider what you would do if you worked less: it could bring you the Beach Life you yearn for.

Great Expectations

'The less routine the more life.'

Amos Bronson Alcott (1799–1888), American philosopher

The room's a little more shabby than you'd like, the sun isn't quite as bright as you'd hoped and, jeez, the crowds! You wanted a little more peace and quiet. But guess what: it doesn't really matter that much because the lazy days languishing under the palm leaves that make up the roof of the beach bar are more than enough to compensate. It doesn't seem to shake you up as it normally would and you actually don't mind so much that the restaurant food's not up to your usual standard. What's going on?

Your familiar high standards have had their sharp edges softened by your letting go of your natural demand for things to be the way you think they should be. Your expectations have come down and you've got a little of the *mañana* going on. It's no bad thing. In fact it's one notion that you can take back home and really emplace in life.

If you think about what's keeping you from getting that holiday feeling at home, so many hurdles are created by your high expectations. Let's look at your home. Do you fret because the house isn't the way you would like it to be? You see how much there is to be done in the house and you won't really settle until the bathroom's sorted out or the garden's finished? There is a tremendous pressure to live perfect lives. The media have a lot to answer for: home-decoration programmes, advertising and programmes that display idyllic interiors, and lifestyles that try to depict a fantasy in a way that seems real. It's hard not to be seduced into thinking that these pictures are somehow real and somehow achievable. But when you're on holiday you are much more accepting of the space around you. It fits for your lifestyle in that week; it is *good enough*.

Another high expectation is that of other people. Boy, is this a big one! Wanting and expecting other people to meet our own expectations is a one-way ticket into a high-stress life. Are you one of those people who anticipate that others will meet their expectations? This can be the cause of much heartache because others strive to meet only their own expectations, not yours. Indeed, they probably don't even know you have an expectation of them. For example, if your personal standard is always to be on time and your friend is always late, then you could struggle if you expect them to behave to your own expectations. Nothing you can do is going to make anyone else change and the angst you put yourself through, fretting about how they've *done it again*, is not going to make any difference.

The stress that goes with inflexible standards can lead to a total dissatisfaction with life. You may end up feeling very frustrated with others and this may come through as seeming unfriendly or 'difficult', which could lead you to loneliness. So what do you do with your high expectations? Well, if you want someone else or something else to be perfect to make you happy, then it's worth identifying what that is and then putting it aside.

For example, if a friend is always late but you want them to be on time, then that is because this will make you feel 'in control': you won't have to change your plans to accommodate his delay. Or, if you think that you cannot ask anyone over to your house until it looks 'perfect', because you will feel anxious if anyone sees it below the standard you wish for your dream house, then that is your anxiety to deal with. In every case of high expectation, you can track it back to your own self-judgements. If the friend *is* late, you can take a Beach Life approach, which is to enjoy the few moments you have to yourself. Likewise, if your house is not up to scratch you can employ radical acceptance, and stay with your insecure emotions until they dissolve. This is what you would do on holiday.

When you mobilise your Beach Life tactics and put them into place, you can reduce your expectations, as you do on holiday, and in turn reduce your stress. If you own up to how many expectations you place on others, you will begin to feel the liberation that comes with not having to control so much of your external world. It is a burden expecting others to be like you – a burden for both you and the people in your life. It can drive them mad, or drive them away. If you lower your expectations you will feel more relaxed and good-tempered, and you may giggle at the things you once thought were so important to you.

Is lowering your expectations lowering standards? No. Lowering your standards is accepting less than you feel is right for you. Lowering expectations is stopping trying to control people, places and things that are out of your control. Lowering expectations helps you to take the heat out of situations that may be causing you personal tension. You don't have to have the perfect outfit or the best car or dine with the right people to feel good. In fact, achieving those things can set you back because you will raise your expectations to a higher point and this will leave you feeling more frustrated.

Employ a little careworn attitude, allow a frayed edge to soothe you and let others be the way they are without feeling out of sorts if it's not going your way. Let this rub off on you and you will become an observer of your own high expectations. You will see them when they march in through the door, even anticipate them, and you will giggle at their futility. Live as though you were swaying in a hammock and watching the sunset go down across the ocean.

Freedom from Fear

'The optimist proclaims that we live in the best of all possible worlds; and the pessimist fears this is true.'

James Branch Cabell (1879–1958), American writer

Is your life a rollercoaster of what-ifs or what-if-it-nevers? Living with fear is so *normal* that you might not even recognise it if it came up behind you and bit you on the bum. Practically every advert you see in the media can be attributed to a covert message that there's 'something to fear'.

- 'Furniture & Fashion Clearance up to 70% off – Hurry!' (The fear is that we're going to miss out on a bargain if we don't get to this shop this weekend.)
- 'Call us for a job done right, first time!' (The fear is that we're going to get a bad job done if we don't.)
- Quick, Get a Better Rate with Us & Beat the Interest Rate Rise! (The fear is that we're going to be done out of a few pounds if we don't switch the mortgage to this company.)

But, because the messages are copious and ongoing, our high tolerance level for this information overload has become normal. It may be 'normal' but it's by no means innate. Check out whether you are running on fear with this simple quick test.

Question	Yes	No
Do you feel anxious when an official-looking letter comes through the door?		
Do you prioritise other people's needs over your own?		
Do you feel a little nervous as you step out of your front door?		
If your ex rings you to get together about something, do you worry what it could be?		
Do you find yourself being sarcastic to others because you can't quite own up to what's bothering you?		
Are you aware of your heart racing at specific things such as being in a social situation or talking with your boss?		
Would you feel nervous going to a party where you didn't know anyone?		
Do you feel panicky if your mobile breaks?		
Do you think sometimes you get frightened when you actually feel sadness or anger underneath?		
Do you hate it when things don't go according to plan?		
When you are talking to others, are you more concerned with what they think of you than what they're saying?		

If you have ticked up to five yeses, you are affected by fear. If you have ticked more than five, you allow fear to rule you.

Our fear levels have changed so much in our modern history and we become agitated at the very essence of modern invention. When we first appeared on this planet, we were hard-wired with the *fear gene*, which provided us with a reliable indication that we were in immediate danger. This kept us safe from predators while we were out hunting for food. Fear produces adrenalin, which provides the extra rush of energy to mobilise us to 'get the hell out of here'. Fear still protects us from imminent danger, even though some types of danger have changed: when we cross a busy road, if someone is threatening us, before we touch an electric wire, if we're walking along a high cliff edge – and so on. We still get the same rush of adrenalin, which tells us when to back off.

But the change that has taken place is that many of us now live with chronic low-level fear that has nothing to do with an imminent threat. It's almost an unknown fear or a hum of anxiety pervading everything. It isn't directed at anything in particular – it's more of a general feeling. It can even manifest itself physically as insomnia, restlessness, lack of concentration or feeling irritable. This type of fear has become so consistent that it's become 'normal'.

It comes in many forms: trepidation, dread, alarm, worry, lack of confidence, nervousness, tension, apprehension, unease. There's a multimillion-pound industry devoted to combating it – hypnotherapy, counselling, neurolinguistic programming, pharmaceuticals, meditation programmes, spas and retreats – and self-help books! People's lives are dominated by it. Because fear assumes there is a potential threat, this leads on to anger and anger leads to pain, which transmutes into more fear. It's an ongoing chain of events in which most of society is caught up.

What is Everyone Frightened Of?

F: false
E: expectations
A: appearing
R: real

Unless you are facing immediate danger, fear is based on what may or may not happen in the future. Because you cannot ever *be* in the future, what you fear is based on pure imagination. From where you are standing now, if you try to imagine what might happen tomorrow, there is a gap of time between the two. In this gap of time anything might happen and so your projection of what might happen tomorrow is based on a fantasy because whatever you think may come true may not come true.

This fantasy is based on – what? That is a difficult question to answer, maybe impossible. What is certain is that our modern society is hugely biased towards the future and this is exposed every second of the day. We have newspaper headlines, television news headlines, Internet exposure and magazines all predicting doom and gloom: 'We're heading for recession', 'Global-warming alert', 'Prices to soar', 'Terror in your city', and so it goes on. It's difficult to avoid the momentum that our universal consciousness moves with these predictions and they are discussed wherever you go.

Let's boil it down to you. You may not worry about these impending disasters but the general low-level fear could transmute itself into you. And let's face it: it's not hard to pick up the *fear baton* and run with it. Mortgage rates, your partner leaving you, getting the sack, debt crippling you. Everyone does it and you'd be hard pressed not to follow suit.

This way of thinking takes you away from that holiday feeling because you are projecting yourself into the future, which is a form of insanity. The gap between now and the time when your projected fear will come true is 'no man's land', which means *no land that man can be in*. It's an illusion, a daydream and a figment of your imagination.

Let's prove this with an exercise.

1. Take a piece of paper and write down five things that create an ongoing fear.
2. Think about them carefully.
3. For how long have you worried about them?
4. Out of the five, how many of them have come true?
5. Which ones have you worried about most yet have never come true?

If the truth is that fears are a figment of your imagination, let's boil them all down to 'the big one' – death. If you are afraid your partner will leave you, the fear transmutes into abandonment, and then death. Should you fear going broke, you might be scared of living on the streets, and then death. If you fear losing others' respect, you'd be unable to 'live with yourself' and then you would face death. But, in the wisdom of the more intelligent mind, this is completely irrational.

All these fears are propagated (1) the insanity of mind racing and (2) the blindness of projecting into the future. But, if you bring yourself into the Stillness, this fear and all others disappear. Once your awareness is gathered and tethered back into the moment, all your imaginary fears fade away. Right now you are alive and you haven't died and you aren't on the point of death or you wouldn't be reading this sentence. The power that fear has on you instantly disappears because it has no hook on which to hang itself.

Every time you feel panickny or anxious, bring your awareness firmly into the Stillness and ask yourself:
What have I got to be afraid of right now?
Not in ten minutes or tomorrow, but right now?

You don't have to be in the Stillness all the time to live free of fear, but just bring yourself back into the moment whenever you remember again. The simple practice of doing this will ease the anxiety and fear itself will drift away because it can no longer survive when you're in the moment. Being in the present moment cuts off fear's food supply and, once this happens, you have set it free and it will sail away. It is such a powerful feeling that you can envisage it as a dark cloud moving away from over you and travelling off towards the horizon. Then the sun will shine down once more and you will become full up with its warmth and light.

COMING HOME: LIBERATION

We all want to be happy and no one has got this market cornered more than children. They live more in the *present* than adults do. If you ask them a question they will answer it directly. For example, an eight-year-old boy was asked by the dentist, who was making conversation while she waited for the dental nurse to prepare some notes, 'So, is it raining outside?' and the boy replied, 'I don't know.' What the dentist was asking was, 'Was it raining when you came in?' but the child answered the question as accurately as anyone would if they were in the moment and that was, 'I don't know because I'm inside.' Interestingly, the younger the child, the more in the moment they are.

As adults we have lost this trait but in 'coming home' we can teach ourselves to relearn this habit. We can be so wrapped up in the future that we forget what it was like to live in the moment, the here and now. When we're in the moment we are at peace and it feels as if we are coming home, home to a peace that we had as children, a stillness and a joy in everyday things. We're more engaged in life, we feel more blissful and we constantly achieve that holiday feeling.

Once you've touched the Stillness you know what it feels like to be at peace with yourself. It's important to make the most of life's quiet times, such as when you're on holiday or by taking time out to quieten your soul and moving into the moment because, when life gets a little tricky, it's harder to *stay* in the moment. If you are threatened with a loss or people politics or some other challenges, you will surely be pulled out of the moment and into mind racing. But there will come a point where you will gain more and more balance as you use the quietness to bring you more and more into the Stillness. And then you will be much less affected by the politics of life. If you spend more and more time in the depths of the ocean, you are less affected by the rough waves on the surface.

In 'Coming Home: Liberation', we look at the final stages in preparation for living life as one long holiday.

Echoes of the Heart

'What we do in life echoes in eternity.'

Gladiator (Ridley Scott, 2000)

The end of your holiday could be about spending the last bit of foreign money on as much cheap booze as you can fit in the case and grumbling about the queues at the check-in desk. Or it could be a moment to adjust things back home while you still have that beach glow and your head in the clouds. You're thinking what a great time you've had and how laid back you feel. You just know you're going to be a *completely different person* when you get back. You won't allow *anything* to bother you. Oh, maybe except . . .

Does your stomach lurch when you think about certain people and situations that linger? It could be the awkwardness you have with your boss or ex, or the extremely overbearing friend that you can't seem to shake off, or you may be dreading a family conflict that you've had going on for years. All these are the Echoes of the Heart.

Once you have established the centre of your life to be seated in the Stillness, you are almost there. From this place you can identify which echoes return to tell you that something needs to be addressed. Have you ever shouted 'hello' in a cave? Within a split second the echo returns your words, over and over again until all you hear is a fading trace. The echo you hear is faint but the source is still you. To quieten your soul you must quieten the Echoes of the Heart.

To find out what your echoes are, imagine your life as a map. There are no examples to illustrate a life map because the words invoke a different picture in everyone's head. Your life map is your life as it is today. If you took a snapshot of your life today, what would the picture look like? In this picture you might sense, feel or see different areas with diverse sensory perception. For example, you might find that there are hot spots and cool spots, vibrant colours or cool colours, calm lines or jagged lines. What you are looking for are the areas that ruffle the whole picture, the distortion or the disturbance. All these areas describe the Echoes of the Heart that return time after time to leave a trace of the past inside you. Once you have found the echo, you will be able to name the scenario or person that you have never released.

The time has come to let them go. If you hang on to old patterns they will hold you back from growing up. Letting them go, however, may be simple but it is definitely not easy. If it were that simple, everyone would be doing it. But, if you want that Beach Life, letting your old patterns go is the final task pending. How much longer do you want to be caught up in the cave where you just cannot help but hear the echo every time it comes round? You can step out of the cave in an instant. There are two things to be done. First, there is the resolution with whom or what you have an outstanding matter with (clearing the decks) and, second, there is the internal adjustment that will not allow further matters to cling to you (becoming transparent).

Clearing the Decks

If you are struggling with life, perhaps you are caught up with your echoes and you are trapped in the cave where you can't *not* hear them. This is because you are clinging to a preferred result – the result that will compromise you. For example, many people live life to gain the approval of another person. This is a life of compromise. Ask yourself,

'Who am I doing this for?' You are listening to the Echo of the Heart as it comes back time and time again to whisper its direction to you. But is this the direction you wish to take? Walking on someone else's road leads you away from your Beach Life and lands you on someone else's desert island.

Make a list of all the people or things that hold you back from walking in a straight line down your road. What echoes do you hear? If they don't perceptibly come to you, then visualise your perfect life as a series of lines, and then identify what it is that you have to go around or jump over to carry on. These are the matters that hold you back and these are the themes that need resolving. It's time to clear the decks.

Now decide whether to take the issue directly to the person. There is one way to decide whether you should do this: if you do, can the situation be changed?

A changeable situation: if you hate your job but you continue with it to please the family, by talking to your family you could discuss alternatives that would fulfil everyone's needs. For example, if you were to become more available to your family – physically and emotionally – due to a shift in work then it could become a win/win scenario.

An unchangeable situation: if you continue your job because of the expectations your parents have of you and because your parents always expected you to do that job but you hate what you're doing, you have to come to terms with the fact that you cannot change your parents and their ideals. Their point of view is an unchangeable situation. You will never change *other people's* perceptions of you, no matter how hard you try. But you can change *yourself* by becoming transparent (see below).

Go through all the things that leave you feeling as if something needs sorting out. And then, one by one, work out what you can change and what you can't change. And, every time you hear an echo, remember: *Don't let anyone live in your head – rent-free!*

Becoming Transparent

Once you have cleared the decks, you can concentrate on not allowing anyone else's 'stuff' cling to you again. To do this, become transparent. Being transparent means just that: your whole essence is transparent and you have no form. If you ever feel the injured innocent and you're thinking, 'How could he/she do this to me?' simply become transparent and allow whatever was said to go right through you.

How does this work? Imagine that you are an outline of a form but in the middle there's nothing on to which any 'hurt' can stick. If you visualise the insult spinning your way like a small comet, it will go straight through you and out the other side. Nothing remains and there is no Echo of the Heart. *It's so simple!* If you don't allow anything to attach itself to you, it cannot affect you. It simply goes right through you. If you practise this every day you will feel the difference instantly.

Let Go

It's a trite saying but it gets right to the point. The idea of letting go is simple in theory but one of the most difficult tasks to undertake. It has been said that the whole purpose of life is to learn to let go – logically straightforward but, oh, so hard to undertake. The reason is that it's scary if you're not confident. But, once you are seated in the Stillness and you have cleared the Echoes of the Heart, it's no longer daunting. So, what is meant by letting go?

Letting go means letting go of resistance: resistance to what *is*. Your resistance to what is is actually holding you back. If you resist the natural ebb and flow of life, then you only make life more difficult for yourself. Imagine you are on a small boat floating down a river along with the current. If you decide to resist the natural flow you will have to paddle the boat to the river bank and hang on to an overhead branch to keep yourself from moving. Hanging on for a while might be manageable but, as soon as you become a little tired, you will wear yourself down. After a while it will take you all your strength to keep your resistance up until that's all you're concentrating on and it becomes painful. You might *have* to let go if your energy runs out, even though you don't want to. When you do let go, there will be a moment of splashing and thrashing until the boat settles back down into the natural flow of the river.

If you let go of resisting the natural flow of life, you will restore your peace of mind and your vision. You will feel more at one with the flow. You will become much more effective at handling difficult situations as you allow 'stuff' to flow through you. The moment you let go, things change. You eradicate fear and conflict. You begin to see your true purpose better, which is to flow with the river. You will become much more creative because you are not halting the flow of new energy from inside out. You will feel lighter and more at ease with the world. By letting go of 'hanging on' you free up physical energy so you feel more vibrant. You become less stressed so you get less ill.

To let go is inspiring and exciting. Here are some examples of how to let go.

Circumstance	What you have done in the past	How to let it go
Fear that your lover will leave.	Tried everything to keep him/her.	In your mind, let them go – accept that nothing you can do can stop them leaving.
Worry about losing your job.	Made yourself ill working long hours.	Accept that your best may or may not be good enough for the job.
Your wayward grown-up child may die of a drug overdose.	Run ragged trying to 'save' them.	Tell them you love them and let them find their own way.

Your mother is constantly criticising you.	Argued with her every time you visit.	Don't visit any more or accept she won't change and become see-through.
You feel bad about being you.	Chronically criticised yourself.	Accept you are not reaching your high standards.

Once you begin to let go, the circumstances that once drove you to despair lose their hold over you. When you let go you're more naturally back into the moment because all your fear of the future coming to a disastrous end has gone.

There are two things to bear in mind through your letting-go experiences.

1. Learn to trust

Glib as this sounds, learning to trust is vital to get the Beach Life. What does this mean? This means coming to recognise that your future will turn out OK. It may not turn out how you want but it will be OK. If you think about being in your boat on the river, it is impossible to see round the next bend. But trust grows when you enter the Stillness because right now everything *is* OK. And that's all you have. Worrying about the future is a kind of insanity, so there is nothing left to do except trust.

2. Be willing to accept your feelings

Do this because projecting into the future is a tool to avoid your feelings. Avoiding feelings helps you to resist the moment. Accept your feelings as they are right now and let them flow through you. Don't judge them or try to rationalise them, just let them be.

Instead of resisting life, become enthralled by the mystery of the universe. Be aware of the unfolding of your life in each moment. Everything is impermanent and any permanence you experience is once again resistance. But remember that all things pass: the drama, the feelings, the problems. Everything passes and, once you recognise that, you will find it easier to release yourself to the flow of life. By letting go you don't do nothing, but you surrender to the flow. You'll find yourself creatively involved in life and what the present moment has to offer, without a struggle.

If you have been going through a crisis, you will experience a very powerful transformation by accepting your feelings. This is a healing process and it is very important to allow this grief to occur and let the emotion come to the surface, without trying to resist, repress or suppress it. This will lessen your fear of the future and bestow enormous strength upon you. A state of crisis can actually lead you to a state of enlightenment as you touch your deepest fears and then let them go. If enlightenment means an all-knowing of the self, then this is what you will touch.

Once you move through this stage, you can reach a certain point where you can simply observe your own thoughts without attaching anything to them. Once you distance yourself and become less fascinated with an outcome, you can rise above it, as if you were on top of a mountain looking down, where you will come to realise that it is all just a story. By moving into the Stillness, you will realise that you have the ability to change that story and to live out a new life that has been set before you.

A New Sense of Power

'All power corrupts, but we need the electricity.'

Unknown

Power – a heady word! It's often attached to a negative charge: power and corruption, nuclear power or applied force. But not in this book. In this book it's a word used to describe something utterly different, something life-changing and quite magnificent.

In the bigger sense of the word, power also describes the energy that is released when new understanding takes place. You may have experienced it in small doses but dismissed it as fleeting. It could have happened on holiday, because a holiday takes you away from your normal environment and unusual senses and perceptions arise because thoughts and stress are at a minimum. But you don't have to be on holiday to recreate this feeling or live life this way. When you open up to the Stillness you begin to see the world in a new way and this will give you a new sense of power: the capacity to bring about change.

Many people live life waiting for something or someone outside themselves to bring about change. They wait in vain for someone to change, someone to recognise them, someone to give them a new job, someone to fall in love with them. Or they wait to own something that will change the way they feel: a new house, car or the winning lottery ticket. All the power for happiness lies in something/someone else's hands and, as long as this power is outside themselves, they have no inner control. When this happens they feel resentful because the world hasn't delivered and has treated them badly. The world has failed them and they are frustrated and desperately unhappy. When you think about it, it is insane. To be waiting for a power outside of yourself to take you into a state of continuous contentment is irrational. You will be waiting for ever!

A sense of a new power comes when you recognise this. That's all it takes: to be aware that nothing outside of you can give you the heart and soul of true contentment. Once you realise this you will gain a new understanding of a power that can feel overwhelming at times, as if the clouds had moved aside and you were seeing the sun for the first time. As soon as you access the Stillness it awakens you to a whole level of experience that you didn't realise was even there. Being in the Stillness manifests into love – for yourself – and, as the love grows inside you, you will notice incredible changes in your outside world.

Unhooking Yourself

When you live in the future, you have to fasten yourself into its potential with 'hooks'. These hooks are clipped on to dreams of what you think will make you happy. These dreams could be that someone you love changes in a way that you will approve of and will finally make your life perfect. It might be that you have saved enough money to move to the place you want to live. It could be that you finally get the recognition from an ex for all the turmoil (their turmoil) you put up with while you were together. Have a look in your mind's eye at what hooks you have fastened on to the future that you believe would transform your life.

By moving into the Stillness you will gain a new strength that will help you unhook yourself from the power these outside influences have on you. It doesn't mean that you don't care: it means that you don't allow them to dominate your wellbeing. As each hook returns to home base, you will feel the power surge within you. The energy that was spent in trying to maintain a hold on other people, places and things can now be invested in the moment. It's exhausting trying to control the uncontrollable. When you stop waiting for the rest of the world to make you feel good you stop acting like the injured party.

Make a list of all the outside influences (people, events or things) you rely on to make you feel good. In your imagination visualise a long, thick rubber band with a hook on the end for each thing that influences you. Can you see the hooks fixed firmly on to each one? Now, unhook them one by one and feel the surge of power that accompanies it. The rubber bands may spring back out again and refasten themselves like triffids. But don't worry: their power has weakened and, the more you stay in the moment, the less it will happen.

The Power of Choice

The power of choice is the *real* power but many of us live as if we had no power at all. We live as if we were in a sailing boat without a rudder and with only the wind in our sails to determine where we go. Where do we end up? We sail to places we don't wish to be. Is it where we really want to be? If you ask someone whether they're happy where they are, the chances are they will say no.

Let's look at your life. Did you choose to be here? You will probably say no – most people do. You didn't end up in the job you hate or the relationship that doesn't work through choice. You ended up in that job or relationship because you didn't know you *had* any other choice. You were consumed with the tradition that you have to put up with things you don't like because 'that's the way it is'. But when you were a young teenager was this the dream you had for yourself? Did you envisage this life at this age? Had you hoped for something different? Do you sometimes ask yourself, 'Where has it gone wrong?'

When you begin to understand that you do have choice, you see things in a different way. Here is a poem that beautifully illustrates this.

I Walk Down the Street
by Portia Nelson

I

I walk down the street.
There is a deep hole in the sidewalk
I fall in.
I am lost . . . I am helpless.
It isn't my fault.
It takes me forever to find a way out.

II

I walk down the same street.
There is a deep hole in the sidewalk.
I pretend I don't see it.
I fall in again.
I can't believe I am in the same place
but, it isn't my fault.
It still takes a long time to get out.

III

I walk down the same street.
There is a deep hole in the sidewalk.

I see it is there.
I still fall in . . . it's a habit . . .
my eyes are open.
I know where I am.
It is my fault.
I get out immediately.

IV

I walk down the same street.
There is a deep hole in the sidewalk.
I walk around it.

V

I walk down another street.

Once you know where the hole in the ground is, there is no longer any reason to fall in it.

Choose Mind Over Matter

You can choose where to be and where to focus your mind every moment of the day. Do you want to be planted in the future or do you want to bring your attention to the fullness and richness of the present moment? Use your mind to bring your awareness back into the present. Focus on your breath or bring your attention into your body. Your body loves your attention; it thrives on it. It glows and energises when your attention is inside it. Feel the warm spot and sense its radiance. Keep nudging your awareness back into the moment. Relish the feeling of wonder and comfort. Bring your attention right into your arms and legs. Feel the movement and warmth, the coolness and solidity.

You have the choice to come back into this moment every time you remember. You will become more and more sensitive to your choices knowing that you can come back to this place any time. Your state of mind will become more attuned to the subtleties of the wonder that being in the moment brings you. You will create a new world for yourself. The sense of the body becomes so subtle that you will get a sense of your cells. You will feel a vibration surrounding them.

From the Inside Out

You will change your sense of self by looking at the different parts of you and what you want. As you bring your awareness more and more into the present, you will gain a perspective. You will be able to see the world objectively rather than feel as if you were an injured party. You will be able to change certain things about yourself in a constructive way rather than a neurotic way.

For example, if you have been in a relationship that doesn't feel right for you, you may be able to see what you need to change in yourself to make the relationship happy rather than wait for the relationship to make you happy. It is so subtle yet so life-changing. From the outside it may seem that nothing has changed in you. But from the inside everything has changed in you.

Choosing the Moment

The only power you really have is to choose to be in the moment. If a thought comes into your mind while you are in the moment, you have the choice to let it bubble up to the surface and dissolve into ripples or allow it to take your awareness out of the present moment. You may ask, 'If this is the only choice I have, isn't it limited?' No, it's liberating.

For example, if you want to get the best job done at a certain time, think of thoughts as tools. If you are painting a wall, you don't want to be encumbered with rags, extra pots of paint and a tub of filler. No, you want one tool: the paintbrush. And you want to hold the paintbrush and focus on putting the paint on the wall, one stroke at a time. That way you maximise the results by focusing on each moment at a time. You can pick up the other tool later, but for now you need only one: the brush. This may seem like a restriction but it isn't: it's the freedom to do the best job possible in the moment that you have.

A Collective Choice

Everyone is working towards happiness. No one works towards being miserable. But, because material gain and politicking are mistaken for happiness, someone has to win and someone has to lose. Everyone grapples to be the winner rather than the loser and *being happy* gets lost in the game. But, of course, happiness doesn't depend on winning or losing or gaining material wealth. Imagine if everybody knew this: wouldn't that be an incredible transformation? If everybody were choosing to find happiness by being in the Stillness, it would become a truly collective choice.

There is a collective choice to be happy and it is possible for *everyone* to be happy. Everyone's happiness is their choice. The more of us who are happy, collectively, the more of us will want to strive for happiness. Everyone can start this course of action right now and that could start with you, because it takes only one match to get the fire going.

Come into the present moment and choose the most effective way to sustain your own personal happiness. Once your fire is burning bright, someone has only to place themselves next to you for your embers to ignite them and then you will both be burning bright. Once their fire is roaring away, there are two of you to ignite others. Imagine if each person ignited another one other person, once a month. After twelve months there would be 2,048 people all burning bright within your community. That is a great example of collective choice.

Pranayama: a Simple Exercise to Feel Your Power

There's a belief in Hinduism that the mind, body and spirit are connected through the breath. And, indeed, breath is life. But how much do we take advantage of the benefits of the breath? In the West, not much. But the power of the breath is astonishing. Did you know that you use only one nostril at a time when you breathe? At any one time, only the right or left nostril will be working. Test it out now.

Place your finger two centimetres below your left nostril for a few seconds, and then under your right. You will know which is working at this moment. Isn't it amazing? Did you also know that the active nostril changes, at regular intervals (approximately an hour and a half) during the day? And that sometimes, for a short time, both nostrils come into play?

The ancient yogis in India knew this and they also knew that there was a powerful connection between the breath and mind. For example, when you are angry, notice your breathing. It will be distressed. When you meditate, notice that your breath becomes calm and shallow. As the ancient yogis were trying to get some control over the mind and this was difficult to master, they realised that by controlling the breath they were better able to influence the mind.

In Hinduism, pranayama is the science of breath control. It consists of series of exercises that are especially intended to meet the body's needs and keep it in vibrant health. Pranayama comes from *prana*, which means life energy, and *ayama*, which means expansion. So, put together, pranayama means breath expansion and control. It was devised to prepare the yogis for meditation by balancing the oxygen and carbon dioxide in the body. This is said to help the body retain energy while meditation takes place.

To practise Pranayama, set aside a few moments and sit quietly. Then do the following.

1. Block your right nostril with your right thumb. Exhale and the breathe in deeply and silently (but not forcefully) through your left nostril.
2. Now block your left nostril with your right middle finger and breathe out and in through the right nostril.
3. Now reverse the process again by blocking your right nostril with your right thumb. Exhale and then breathe in deeply and silently (but not forcefully) through your left nostril.
4. And now block your left nostril with your right middle finger and breathe out and in through the right nostril.

Repeat the above process for 4–5 minutes once or twice a day. It's important there are no gaps between the breathing. As you practise this powerful breathing technique, be aware of your breath as it goes in and comes out. If you drift off into thought, gently come back to your breathing and feel the rhythm and flow as you gently breath and relax. This exercise will bring you back to your centre.

It is said that this technique teaches us the way to breathe. We have become too used to breathing into our chest and this inhibits the amount of oxygen we get, which, in turn, impedes our wellbeing. More oxygen to the brain helps us fight stress and relaxes us. A relaxed mind and body help us to stay focused, give us clearer mental vision and promote more peace of mind.

Make friends with your breath. It will be inside you for a long time. You may as well work with your breath by encouraging it into your body rather than pushing it away from your body. This will help to gain a new sense of power, which is focused on the power within rather than handing the power over to forces without.

Come back into your body again, right now. Can you feel your body re-energising as it bathes in your attention? Can you feel each cell vibrate as you worship it?

The Science of Joy

'Only one thing made him happy, and now that it was gone, everything made him happy.'

Leonard Cohen, Canadian singer-songwriter, poet, novelist

In this world, you get a prize for just showing up – joy! It's your birthright. From time to time you can expect a well of joy to fill your heart and lift your spirits. Sometimes it happens for good reasons and sometimes there's just no rhyme nor reason to it, it just happens.

Joy pays no heed to rationalisation or appropriateness. Sometimes it does its own thing and arrives without any warning at all. It can happen when you're having a rough time or when you feel down and depressed. It can happen when you're delirious with happiness.

There's no logic to it. It can take place when you have a conversation with a six-year-old girl who's telling you the things she'd save if her house were on fire and why the guinea pig would come before her dad. Or when you realise that, as you've been walking down the street, you've absent-mindedly been playing 'avoid the cracks'. Or it can happen when you catch the eye of a kind old woman who gives you a smile radiating warmth and cosiness. Or you suddenly see the sinking sun, teetering on the horizon like a big, fat, wobbly melon, and it takes your breath away. All you know is that it was a small thing that transported you into a state of complete personal fulfilment in a nanosecond.

Achieving joy is seldom about personal achievements or reaching goals. In fact it's the *mystery* of joy that is so enrapturing. The mysterious thing is that you become captivated by the ordinariness of life that unfolds in that precise moment. And the way joy bursts through even when you are dreading a meeting or feeling flattened by a break-up only adds to the allure.

Even the cynical experience joy. There's no finer moment than when a surge of joy bursts up in moments of pessimism or situations of self-pity. It's like nature's reward for putting up with the nonsense. Even the most depressive situations can trigger a gush of joy: the joy of surrendering, for instance, when you feel so depressed and give up on the world, so you take yourself to bed, then snuggle under the blankets and not care one jot about the rest of the world. Delicious!

It's a peculiar thing the way the world chases after all the things that don't supply joy. The house of your dreams can give you pleasure but it can't bring you joy. A fabulous pair of shoes can temporarily satisfy you – but they won't bring you joy. We all work to buy things that we think are the answer to our dissatisfaction, but they're not. The irony is that the more you have, the more it could divert you from joy. If you constantly experience the 'high' of clinching the deal or spending the cash, then through sheer repetition and habit you might think that that's the only place to find joy. Are you postponing life's rich reward until you make enough money or clinch the right deal?

The science of joy is simple. You don't have to go to great lengths to reap life's number-one gift. And, you can get joy in an instant. Practise it now.

Sit quietly for a moment . . .
Bring your awareness on to your breath.
Can you hear your thoughts?
Don't push them away, just watch them.
Watch them come into your mind and then leave again.
Feel your body . . .
It comes alive when you bring your attention into it.
Your body loves your attention . . .
Use your senses to their maximum . . .
Let your eyes show you colour . . .
Let your nose tantalise you with scents . . .
Let your fingers brush a surface . . ..
Rest up . . .
Bring your awareness back into the moment.

Ask yourself a question: what brings me joy? Do you notice how you feel agitated when your mind jumps into action? When you agitate the mind, the emotions also feel agitated.

So don't ask. Forget the question. Just be in the moment.

It is the absence of any questions that brings joy.

Isn't that what happens on holiday? You stop asking yourself why, what, who, how when? You may think it's because you have 'escaped' from normal life that you feel wonderful. That's true because in your normal life you ask yourself hundreds of questions that you cannot possibly answer. They only create stress. But what you've done is stopped asking.

So, for this moment, simply don't ask yourself any questions. Joy happens when the surface of the lake is still.

The art of joy is to recognise that the things you think will bring you joy will become traps if they become fixed as your goals. What if you couldn't get them, then what? Does that mean no joy for you? You may become anxious that you won't achieve your goals or, if you do achieve them, you may become fearful that your achievements will be taken away from you. Money and success – do they bring you joy? No, they bring you money and success. Fame and power – do they bring you joy? No, they bring you fame and power. You don't need money, success, fame or power to experience joy. They are not related.

For now, don't fret about this question. Bring your awareness back on to your breath and your attention into your body . . . relieve your mind of questions . . . let the ripples of the lake fade into the edge of the shore . . . feel the deepness once more

If you pose yourself many questions, this will trouble your emotions. Why? Why not? Why not now? Why not me? These are questions the mind cannot answer and they raise troubled emotions: anxiety, grasping, fear, uncertainty, sadness, shame. The ripples of the lake are disturbed as the winds create waves and the water slaps against the shore.

Bring an end to the questions . . . calm the waves on the lake . . . let the ripples move to the edge of the shore once more . . . bring your attention back on to the breath . . . feel the body . . . calm the emotions . . . joy remains ever still in the deepness.

The Art of Nonattachment

Do you feel joy, lightness and ease in what you are doing? When you're on holiday those feelings prevail. Each day is a joy and you flow with life and life flows with simplicity and both need very little effort. *You* haven't changed and life hasn't changed but something else has definitely changed. Perhaps it's the wishing to be in the present moment that underlines your day. You will probably be giving the present moment your full attention, not wishing to be anywhere or anyone else. You're not concerned with results and outcomes as you let go of the future.

Do you want joy but seem so far away from it? It's not so far away.

It's within your reach and there's one piece of know-how that will get you there: nonattachment.

*Non*attachment is not *de*tachment: it's something quite different. Detachment describes a state in which a person overcomes his or her attachment. To detach from someone or something you have to have been attached to them in the first place. Both words imply being 'stuck to' and becoming 'unstuck from'. Many people live in a seesaw of attachment and detachment in terms of relationships, goals, work, etc. Nonattachment is something else.

Practise nonattachment now

Think about what worries you. Do you feel unsure, confused and angry? Do you feel in danger of losing something? You may feel a sense of foreboding or a sense of loss, but these feelings are attached to wishing and yearning that things were different. And this leads to feelings of discontentment.

Instead, bring your mind awareness back on to your breath . . . bring your attention into the body . . . feel the vibrancy of your body as it receives your attention . . . feel the safety in the present moment . . . here it is safe and it is your real home . . . let your troubled feelings pass . . . accept this moment as it is . . . it is perfect . . .

You are not attaching your joy to any thing or person outside yourself. And, because of this, there is a distinct absence of troubled emotions, including an absence of desire.

The irony of nonattachment is that, as you let go of the very thing you are grasping on to, it is still yours. To illustrate this, if you pour sand into your hand and try to grasp it, it escapes. But, if you simply hold your hand out and let the sand fall into your palm, it stays.

If you are so afraid of losing your lover that you cling on with all your power, your actions will push the other person away from you. If you let them go and allow them to be, they are more likely to stay. By realising that everything has an impermanence, you can afford to release your grip on attachment. Yes, at first it may feel as though you are losing out and you will end up with nothing. But life will show you that the opposite is true and you will gain more joy. If you don't believe this, it's only because you haven't yet had the experience.

There is a wonderful fable that illustrates this. It's an anonymous tale called 'The Tiger, the Man, the God'.

A man was being chased by a tiger. He ran as hard as he could until he was at the edge of the cliff with the tiger in hot pursuit. The man looked over the edge of the cliff and saw a branch growing out of the side of the cliff a few feet down. He jumped down and reached the branch just as the tiger reached the edge of the cliff. The tiger growled viciously as the man sighed a great sigh of relief.

Just then, a mouse came out from a crevice and began to chew on the branch. The man looked down to what was a drop of a thousand feet and sure death and looked to the heavens and yelled out, 'Oh, God, heaven's above, if you are there, please help me. I will do anything you ask, but please help!'

Suddenly a voice came booming down from heaven. 'You will do anything I ask?' it questioned.

The man, shocked to hear a reply to his question, yelled back, 'I will gladly do anything you ask, but please save me!'

The voice from heaven then replied, 'There is one way to save you but it will take courage and faith.'

The branch began to weaken from the mouse's attentions and the tiger was still growling a few feet above the man, 'Please, Lord, tell me what I must do and I will do it. Your will is my will.'

The voice from heaven then said, 'OK, let go of the branch.'

The man looked down to a fall of a thousand feet and certain death. He looked at the mouse still chewing on the branch and up at the hungry tiger a few feet away. Then he looked up at the heavens and screamed, 'Is there anyone else up there?'

If you are holding on for dear life, like the man in the fable, your attachment may have got you into some deep trouble.

Practising nonattachment may feel frightening at first but simply bring yourself back into the Stillness by focusing on the breath . . . bring your attention into the body . . . feel the vibrancy inside . . . can you sense the safety of the present moment once more? This is the science of joy and the art of nonattachment.

Laugh with Life

'Humour is the great thing, the saving thing. The minute it crops up, all our irritations and resentments slip away and a sunny spirit takes their place.'

Mark Twain (1835–1910), American author

Laughter is life's tonic. In fact we call those people who make us laugh 'a real tonic'. The benefits of laughing at life include reducing stress, relieving pain and producing the feel-good hormones. Laughter wards off depression and makes you sleep better. What's there not to laugh about?

Being able to see a funny side in every situation keeps the lightness in life. Great speakers are the ones who make you laugh, but the best speakers are those who make you laugh at them. Not taking yourself seriously brings you on to the lighter side of life.

To illustrate this, let's take kids as an example. Who'd have 'em? They wind you up, stress you out and have you running around in circles. Have you ever had a situation where the child is having an almighty tantrum in the shop, the teenager's looking for his under-wear in the fridge or you shut the windows so your neighbours can't hear you shouting at the top of your voice? We've all done it.

But, instead of collapsing in a heap of 'Life can't go on like this!', look at it another way. Kids are drunks. They are born completely inebriated; they can't do anything for themselves. What they do well is poo, cry and throw up. By the time they're walking they're creating a trail of devastation while bumping into everything. They fight you every inch of the way with tantrums, screaming and general defiance. Gradually, the drunkenness wears off until the teenage years, when they are suffering from one long hangover as they grunt, sulk and generally act as if someone had done them in. See kids as drunks and it goes a long way towards better managing the drama.

Take a couple of steps back and watch your whole life as a drama on stage. You get a little distance, which puts you in touch with your *real life* underneath all of life's dramas. There is humour in everything. Even going to the supermarket is funny with the bun fight around the assistant who's putting 'reduced' labels on foods and the wisecracks on the Tannoy system as a member of staff goes off on one.

And, best of all, laugh at yourself. There's nothing funnier than seeing your own tantrums and hiccups as a series of sketches. It bends the inflexibility of self-importance while illuminating the truth. After all, always being right actually smacks of arrogance with barriers of should, ought and mustn't. And no one likes anyone who takes themselves too seriously.

Here's a joke to make you laugh. Two businessmen in London were sitting down for a break in their soon to be new store. As yet, the store was not ready, with only a few shelves set up. One said to the other, 'I bet any minute now some stupid tourist's going to walk by, put his face to the window, and ask what we are selling.'

No sooner were the words out of his mouth than, sure enough, a curious Scotsman walked to the window, had a peep in, and in a broad Scottish accent asked, 'What're you selling here?' One of the men replied sarcastically, 'Idiots!' Without skipping a beat, the Scotsman said, 'Ye're doing well – only two left!'

When you laugh, you fill yourself up with the nourishment of the Stillness and you feel less and less the need to be right. Instead, what you feel is the desire to be present. You will see humour in everything that happens – yes, even the seeming tragedies. It will free you up and help you get that Beach Life feeling. After all, life is one long party.

Enjoying the View

'When you are watching the view, you are there.'

Anonymous

Have you ever had the occasion, while on holiday, when you take a moment to savour the view and, suddenly, everything in your life seems to fall into its rightful place? It's as if blinkers had been removed from your eyes and for the first time you can see. Everything is clear and crisp and fresh. It's a physically powerful feeling and one that may have taken you by surprise. This is what's known as 'the view'.

The view is a profound and blissful state, which gives you a glimpse of your real life under your mental chatter. Your enemies become insignificant and your problems become meaningless. It's a moment of awakening and you will know exactly when you have arrived. You can remain there for as long as you want without doing anything out of the ordinary. You effortlessly flow with life. You can see how many of your previous efforts to achieve and make happen were futile. But your future is clear and you are content to follow the path of least resistance.

You feel a well of compassion and wisdom and this is directed to yourself first and others second, because you know that you, yourself, are your first priority. But the compassion shines out of you in a way that feels different from before because you know that others have their own paths to follow.

While enjoying the view you notice that a profound sense of humour is bubbling inside you and you see how nonsensical life is. You visualise the laughing Buddha because you now understand where his giggles are emanating from. It's as if all the doubts of your chattering mind have been dispelled in one fell swoop and you realise that life's been playing a joke on you and you have finally got it.

You finally understand all that searching that you've been doing, trying to be happy, has brought you to this point and 'this is it'. There is no other place because the view is the place to be. And, as you stand on the hilltop and gaze around you, you can see that the clouds come and go as all problems come and go. Even though some clouds are big black ones and some are little fluffy ones, they all come and go at the same pace; attaching any meaning to them is pointless. Resolving problems in order to enjoy the view is like trying to clean the house so you can learn how to ride a bike – the two aren't related.

While taking in this magnificent view you will also become aware that pinning happiness on to 'highs' is a futile exercise because these are simply mental gossip. You see these highs as distractions from the view. They fulfil a different part of you and you can enjoy them without *needing* them to make you feel happy. Your goals, plans and ambitions are still there but they don't grip you the way they once did. They are important but your happiness doesn't depend on them and you can let any surrounding anxiety dissolve like footprints in the sand being washed away by the waves.

At the same time, you will recognise that when you're enjoying the view you don't need to jump in and mess around with whatever you are taking pleasure in. For example, if you walk into a beautiful garden that takes your breath away, you don't need to pick all the flowers and take them home to recreate the same experience in your house. You simply breathe in the joy of that moment and feel its wonder in the same way a child would; it's enough to sustain you for a length of time. The more you breathe in the moment, the more you feel the bliss. As your psyche experiences more and more bliss it will naturally lean towards the place where bliss is unbounded. The more you experience the view, the more you will be drawn towards it.

And the more you enjoy the view, the more contented you will become. As your contentment increases, your intrinsic worth flourishes. This is to say that the true essence of your nature will become harmonised and will manifest itself in love, tolerance, compassion and appreciation of others. This becomes the centre of you and the position from which you will view the world. It's a new type of autonomy where you feel that you are swimming with the flow of life rather than swimming against it. Your creativity will become astonishing and you will tap into an intelligence that you knew you had but you couldn't quite get to. You will find that your aspirations don't seem so far away.

If you just notice, you will see that you always enjoy the view. Oh – except when you think there's something else you should be taking care of before you can get back to the view again. The fact is, you simply keep busy most of the time. Still, it doesn't take much effort to get back to the view. In fact, the less effort you use the better. It's the being busy and doing too much that keep you distracted, but being in the moment or taking the view will bring you straight back to that lush paradise.

If your conditioning says that happiness will be realised on an ongoing basis only when 'I achieve . . .' or when 'I have . . .', all it takes is to be aware of those thoughts and, just for a minute, step away from them and watch them from a distance. Just becoming aware that you are having those thoughts is enough to bring you back into enjoying the view.

Once you've got that cracked, the next step is to teach yourself to enjoy the view when you're in the company of others. When you have cracked that one, you have become a Master of life. Few people ever achieve it, but what better life purpose could you possibly have?

Liberation

'The true value of a human being can be found in the degree to which he has attained liberation from the self.'

Albert Einstein (1879–1955), German-born physicist

'Liberation' – a powerful and provocative word. You can see it in your mind's eye. Someone standing on top of a hill with their arms held out wide and their head looking to the sky while shouting for joy; or a set of ski tracks in the middle of a wild territory in Greenland; or a hammock slung between two palm trees jutting out from a white-sand beach and miles of deep blue ocean.

In more down-to-earth terms, liberation can be summed up as feeling completely unconstrained or en-lightened, as in *lightened up*. It's not attainment or something to 'work for', because it's always been there, but maybe you didn't know it. It's more of a letting go than attaining something that brings you liberation. A letting go of the 'when I get there then I'll be happy'. Enlightenment means 'knowing', and, once you know that letting go is where it's at, you really do 'know'.

And what do you know? You know the universal truth that everyone has the opportunity to feel liberated. In one sense, it was simple, pure luck that you went looking and discovered the freedom that was always there, just under the surface. Now you know where it is, you can tap into it as and when you want. Once you've experienced the Stillness, it's hard to ignore, because it suddenly offers a depth to life that presents many answers to the questions you've been asking. And, once you've touched the Stillness, it really is the start of a new beginning.

The Six Key Elements to Liberation

1. Not being ruled by mind racing

To be no longer ruled by your racing thoughts is a powerful path to feeling liberated. By not associating your 'self' with your fettered mind, and creating an opening between the two, you will find liberation waiting for you. Your heart will soar as you recognise this is the true path to freedom.

2. Letting go

So often you want happiness and freedom but so often the place you look for it is fruitless. You have been made to believe that if you 'let go' of trying to 'make it' you will end up with nothing. But nothing could be further from the truth. In fact, the opposite is true. The more you let go, the more freedom you achieve.

You let go of two things:

- constantly wanting and wishing for things you don't have; and
- constantly wishing that you didn't have what you've got.

By accepting that everything in this moment is just the way it is meant to be, you have liberated yourself from the negative fantasies that

161

accompany wishing and yearning. Anyone anywhere can feel liberated by just doing this one thing.

3. Radical acceptance

By radically accepting things as they are right now, you are co-operating with the movement of life. When you accept things that you had considered unwelcome, life's meaning unravels itself. Radical acceptance will allow life's greater good to be revealed to you. You will become open to the wonders that lie underneath 'bad' or 'negative' emotions or experiences. There is always an underlying purpose to any situation, if only to help you to find peace instead of conflict by stepping back from your emotional drama. By saying yes to the moment, you are radically accepting what is happening without trying to alter anyone else or anything else. This is an incredible freedom.

4. Discipline

Incorporated into radical acceptance is the notion of self-discipline. What does that mean? It means to recognise and acknowledge craving, without bowing to it. Do you crave things that you think will make your life perfect: a bigger home, a better job, a perfect lover, a glass of wine, the next cigarette? But you know that you cannot ever fill up the hole inside that creates the craving? Overcoming cravings through self-discipline will bring liberation.

As you feel the craving, a kind of magnetic pull towards something outside yourself, you can feel the force behind it, pulling you forwards. Instead, sit with the craving and become aware of it inside you. See the energy beaming out of you towards the thing you crave, like a vibrant rope light, and keep your attention on it. The more you focus your attention on this energy field the more you will dissolve the craving. Radically accepting the craving is the way to get to the heart of it as quickly as the speed of light. There is no quicker route.

Emotional and physical cravings create stress in the nervous system. By using this technique of self-discipline you are calming your nervous system in the fastest possible way. You will reap the rewards from the first time you practise self-discipline in this way. Why? Because you have radically accepted that something outside of you had a pull on you, but you have chosen to resist.

5. The art of being

The art of being is being able to understand that underneath life's drama there is a whole ocean of existence that is available to us whenever we want to dive down into its unlimited potential for happiness. Once this is understood, it is possible to live life with humour and joy.

The key to the art of being is the integration of the Stillness with everyday life. It's your complete presence in whatever you do. Practise it and weave it into your daily life like a regular meal. You will notice a subtle transformation between your mind, body and spirit. You will become aware of the pervading life that sits underneath your life's drama. You will recognise that you don't need to change anything to practise the art of being. But transformation will happen as a result of your putting these changes in place. And you will have that blissful holiday feeling every day.

6. Living a goalless life

Finally, liberation means living a goalless life. Quite simply, it's about living for the moment and not throwing out the present for the future, which, incidentally, never comes. You know the standard acronym, SMART, standing for: Specific, Measurable, Achievable, Results-oriented, Time-based. It's a standard for winning or losing. But there's a new twenty-first-century shift that's challenging these old ways. What was once 'You have to set goals and achieve them to be happy' is changing. Look at it this way: do you want your epitaph to read, 'Tried hard, achieved loads, but *boy* was he washed out at the end!' Or would you prefer, 'He lived life as if he were always on one long holiday.'

To be liberated means:

Life's a beach

- never having to ask – 'What am I doing with my life?';
- understanding you're part of something bigger;
- knowing you're on the right road;
- taking life seriously;
- having a brainstorm of an idea but not wanting to follow it up in case it distracts you from being here;
- putting problems away;
- laughing at the sheer absurdity of life;
- learning to not overstretch;
- not having to live in the mountains meditating, but . . .
- . . . living a modern life, in balance;
- understanding what is meant by 'adulthood';
- knowing you have real choice;
- appreciating that peace can be found through discipline;
- profoundly recognising that material things don't bring joy;
- becoming the student;
- being able to see life panoramically, not just ahead of you;
- living a simple life;
- seeing the world in colour;
- knowing that loving others starts with loving yourself;
- not feeling responsible for others;
- knowing nothing is permanent;
- knowing everything you do counts;
- understanding that you don't know what you are going to think or feel in the future . . .
- . . . and being OK with that;
- reassessing;
- being accountable to yourself;
- letting go; and
- living as if every day were a holiday.

INDEX